Claiming the Corner

Becoming a Kingdom Impact
Church Jesus' Way

Mark Schoenhals

WESTBOW
PRESS®
A DIVISION OF THOMAS NELSON
& ZONDERVAN

WestBow Press books may be ordered through booksellers or by contacting:

WestBow Press
A Division of Thomas Nelson & Zondervan
1663 Liberty Drive
Bloomington, IN 47403
www.westbowpress.com
844-714-3454

ISBN: 978-1-6642-2837-5 (sc)
ISBN: 978-1-6642-2836-8 (hc)
ISBN: 978-1-6642-2838-2 (e)

Library of Congress Control Number: 2021906095

Print information available on the last page.

WestBow Press rev. date: 04/24/2021

CONTENTS

ACKNOWLEDGEMENTS

Special thanks to all those who have been an encouragement in the producing of this work through prayer, suggestions, and edits, especially: Matthew O'Brien, Sherrill Morris, Suzanne Tietjen, Emily Schoenhals, Sharon Schoenhals, Pastor Joel Goff, Rev. Christopher Marchand, Pastor Phil Formo, Pastor Brian Goke, Pastor Mark McCready, Pastor Jim Powell, Cameron Mott, the leaders of Living Waters Church, and many more.

In loving memory of Rev. Arnold and Ilse Conrad for the Kingdom Impact they made on their corner.

What readers are saying about
Claiming the Corner:

Claiming the Corner: Kingdom Impact Jesus' Way gives us a fresh perspective on Jesus' parables that will both challenge and inspire pastors and church leaders. Mark helps us rethink what mission and ministry look like in a culture where the old church paradigms no longer work. However, instead of offering yet another model for ministry to adopt, we are invited to bring about the Kingdom by seeing our communities through Jesus' eyes and to walk in the way he taught us.

—Chris Marchand Anglican pastor and author
of Celebrating the 12 Days of Christmas:
a guide for churches and families

If you are satisfied to be just another church on the corner, do not read this book. If your primary goal in ministry is to grow your church, do not consider the contents of this book. If you would like to make a name for you and your congregation, read no further. However, if your call is to grow the Kingdom of God, serve sacrificially, and push the boundaries for discipleship in Jesus Christ, you need to read this book – cover to cover – with your entire leadership team. Pastor Mark dares to re-examine the Kingdom parables of Jesus as recorded in Matthew 13 through the missional lens of leaving your church walls. You will be challenged. You will be stretched. And you will be blessed as the Holy Spirit moves through your ministry to the dark corners in your community. Fasten your seatbelt for real Kingdom Impact!

—Pastor Brian Goke, Faith Lutheran, Bloomington,
IL (Lutheran Congregations in Mission for Christ)

Pastor Mark Schoenhals looks through the lens of this parable of the sower (and a few others) to challenge any church, whether large and thriving or aging and declining, to imitate the way Jesus related to those around Him. Any church, no matter its make-up, can open their church doors, see the needs of their neighbors, and show them the love of Christ. Pastor Schoenhals shares the real-life experiences of several churches who did just that.

I was encouraged by those stories and, more than once, moved to tears. Claiming the Corner: Seeking Kingdom Impact Jesus' Way offers practical examples of Kingdom work done by ordinary people led and empowered by God. This book is so timely and very needed. Highly recommended!

—Suzanne Davenport Tietjen, speaker and author of: The Sheep of His Hand: Reflections on the Psalms from a 21st Century Shepherd, and 40 Days to your Best Life for Nurses.

Each week a pastor seeks to end the weekly sermon with a personal challenge and application suggestion. In "Claiming the Corner", Pastor Mark Schoenhals unpacks the parables of Matthew 13 with a congregational focus. Each chapter gives a real-life illustration of how a local church is living out the implication of the parable in their own community. Also included are questions for church leadership to work through together.

Fresh, down to earth, practical, this resource provides great leadership discussion questions and a helpful group process for churches to effectively narrow their focus on real ministry opportunities locally. This is a practical "how to" for churches that seek to minister in the good soil God has already prepared around them.

—Rev. Joel Goff - Converge Worldwide pastor

The challenge of any evangelical congregation is to share the Gospel through not only what is proclaimed from the pulpit, but what is experienced through a congregation's outreach. Rather than well-meaning words, Pastor Schoenhals illustrates a ministry through action by meeting the needs of local communities. Claiming the Corner: Seeking Kingdom Impact Jesus' Way, illustrates strategies that have changed communities for the sake of the Gospel in both Argentina and in one American city. The author's passion for the Gospel is an inspiration for all who read this book. Like Jesus' ministry, these pages speak of reaching to the forgotten, the often ignored.

—Rev. Philip Formo, Pastor and Author.

Anyone who closely follows 95Network knows how much value we place on creating practical resources to help small and midsize churches. The practical application of Jesus' parables to engage and ignite the fires of evangelism and discipleship in *Claiming the Corner* lays out a simple solution to help any congregation reach their community. Simply put, the mission of every church puts action to their stated reason for existing. Mark teaches us that being Jesus to a lost and dying world isn't about just shouting the Gospel . . . it's actually more about serving others we interact with every day."

—Dale Sellers – Executive Director 95Network,
Author of *"STALLED: Hope & Help For Pastors
Who Thought They'd Be There By Now"*

INTRODUCTION: SETTING THE STAGE

"Is this going to be just another Lutheran church on the corner?" Maybe you have asked this type of question as a pastor, church leader, or as a church member, concerned for your congregation's mission. Remove Lutheran and insert your <u>own</u> denomination, (or non-denomination), and you will get a sense of the dilemma I faced seven years into my call at my current church. We had been a new mission start, having formed out of a doctrinal dispute with a large denomination. Excitement and energy were tangible at the beginning, we enjoyed the freshness of new faces, new surroundings, and new leaders. Initially, lay leaders were energized, serving on interim leadership teams, etc. There was much busyness needed in those first months to make the new mission work, especially as people from four different local congregations comprised the new membership.

But what followed is a more common story: After the initial growth and honeymoon period, we were no longer the new church on the block. Quickly, we plateaued in growth. Behind the growing malaise was the fact that the church's initial vision had been accomplished. A new congregation had been planted based on what most of the members and attenders wanted. *But now what?* We were just another church, in a very "churched" community, looking for what every other church was looking to do — to grow, which is what churches are supposed to do, right?

One summer Sunday, I was looking out over the congregation

of familiar faces. Many people were away on vacation, and with so many pews empty, it looked as though we were back to the same "originals" we had at the beginning. I stood there with a sinking feeling in my stomach. It confirmed what I had been feeling for some time already. The air was leaking out of the balloon. It felt as though God was giving me a window into the future based on the current trajectory. Was this all the busyness was intended to be? Was this going to be just another Lutheran church on the corner?

We got busy (again) and hired a helpful consultant (95network), and we learned of our need to clarify our mission and vision for a new season and trim the number of ministries and annual events we had inherited from our four "feeder" congregations. We had 75 ministries and events for a church of 150. The busyness had actually become a busy-mess! We said goodbye to some traditional programs that had outlived their shelf life. With those decisions made, some of them hard, we emerged from that consulting process with a new, streamlined mission statement, and a clarified target for outreach — young adults and young families. For the second time since the congregation formed, there was a clearly stated mission and a renewed commitment by our leadership to pull toward that goal.

Fueled by this vision process, we put our shoulders to the plow to reach a local neighborhood that was largely unchurched compared to the surrounding area. We saw a tripling of our youth and children's ministries, with conversions and baptisms along the way. But along with that, came a whole new list of problems associated with loving and assimilating wonderfully complex unchurched folks into what had been a middle-aged, middle-class congregation.

If this book was presenting a model for church growth, that would be the end of the story. There are many good processes like the one we used to create a culture of mission buy-in and growth potential. But in some cases, it can just lead to a church that is just a little bit larger, sometimes simply taking people from other local congregations who are attracted to the vision. Let us be clear, *that is not the mission of Jesus!* And, by the way (spoiler alert) after a few years of expansion in our children's and youth ministries, our church was really no larger than it had been before. Some of us were left wondering: Had we had done something wrong?

The purpose of this book is to ask this question: What does God really want churches to do? Is our quick assumption that he just wants them to grow, accurate or even Biblical? How does Jesus measure Kingdom Impact? Here is an even better question: *How can my congregation learn to make Kingdom Impact in the world the way Jesus instructed?* Jesus gives us the answer to all these vital questions in his six Kingdom parables in Matthew 13.

Beyond Church Growth

Back to the original question that I faced seven years into my tenure at my current congregation, even after a renewed sense of mission: *Is this all this is supposed to be?* Here are all the follow up questions that go down a rabbit hole of discouragement: *Will this be just another congregation on the corner looking to grow... just like every other church on every other corner? Aren't there some towns that have too many churches already? Isn't that part of the problem? How many bodies of Christ does God need in one area, all doing basically the same thing?*

Here is the amazing, grace-filled answer: No, there are not too many! God wants "His" church on every corner. Not my church, not your church, not a church from this fellowship, or with this association, or this style of worship or preaching, but <u>His</u> church. If your question is: "Is this just going to be another (*insert your fellowship or denomination*) church on the corner?", let me direct you to the "question behind the question": How does <u>*my*</u> church become <u>*God's*</u> church on <u>*this*</u> corner?

I believe this is one of the most important questions facing the Christian Church right now, especially in the post-quarantine era. I also believe that the best person to answer that question is Jesus.

This is his mission after all, and he is the expert on the impact the Kingdom is designed to make.

In Matthew 16:18, Jesus promised that against his church the gates of hell would not prevail. This means Jesus' Church will lay siege to those gates and force its way through, just as Jesus did in his death upon the cross, to force his way through those gates and deal with the enemy on his own turf. If that is true, to be Jesus' Church today we must embody the sacrificed and resurrected life of Jesus on every corner, even the most hellish ones, right on that turf.

So, what did Jesus say about this Church? (The church that is his and not ours; the church that is a mission rather than a country club; the church that does not see itself as competing against the other churches in town). Jesus presents that vital answer to all these questions in his Kingdom parables.

A Snapshot of a Kingdom Impact church in Azul, Argentina.

It was April in the Southern Hemisphere. A former congregation I served had sought out a new kind of global mission partnership that was just becoming popular at the time: a church-to-church partnership supporting a local mission project. It did not mean just becoming a financial partner, giving money through a larger mission organization to fund many projects around the world. Instead, this meant a congregation-to-congregation partnership, one church in the global south and one in the global north. From the congregation in the global south came the idea and the leadership to meet the needs of their community. They did the research; they provided the drive and the model. From the congregation in the global north came the financial backing and the moral and spiritual support to keep the mission going. Cementing this relationship was the vital first mission visit, from the north to the south, congregational members serving under the leadership of the southern church, working shoulder to shoulder with them and understanding the context of the mission to which they were contributing — now adding their hands and feet to the work. When first envisioned decades ago, the model was termed "accompaniment".

So, there I was in Azul, Argentina, meeting some of the most beautiful people I had ever encountered, the 14 members of *Iglesia Luterana de la Transfiguración*, (Transfiguration Lutheran Church). This congregation was started in the mid-1800s by missionaries to serve German-speaking immigrants. It had now dwindled to 14 people representing 3 families. Any outside assessment would have concluded that this congregation was dying, especially when compared to the old photos they had of the church 80 years ago when there were 400 to 500 members. Now they were 14. But inside this remnant beat a passionate heart to reach a community of 3000 people living in poverty on the edge of town, some dwelling in makeshift shelters, lacking water, and electricity, and heating their homes with wood and other combustibles during the cold, damp South American winters. Their passion was especially for the preschool children of those families who often entered kindergarten lacking school-readiness, appropriate dress, and proper nourishment. The members of Transfiguration Lutheran knew in their hearts that with the resources of a willing partner, they could build a childcare center that would provide school-readiness education and healthy food. This would allow both parents in those families to find work during the day, knowing their kids were cared for in a loving, Christian environment. For the most disadvantaged, the care would be offered for free. But for those who could contribute even one peso a month, a vital and dignity-building investment would be collected to support the ministry.

All they needed was a partner to make it happen. An amazing mission organization, Lutheran Partners in Global Mission, had found that partner, and it was us, a mid-sized congregation in the Minneapolis area looking to "do" mission in some other part of the world. We had no idea what we were getting into and what life-changing experiences we would have as part of this mission accompaniment. Together we built *Sol y Esperanza* Childcare Center, serving initially 30 and soon 60 precious preschoolers and their families.

One April afternoon, I took a walk from the newly built childcare center into the community it served. As I walked, simple, but well-built concrete homes gradually became drafty dwellings and shacks made with whatever materials people could find. As I went deeper into the community, the power lines vanished, and a few open wells appeared. Cars were replaced by horses and goats. It was like travelling back in time. As I journeyed, the mysterious and energizing presence of the Holy Spirit drew near. Here is what I had been thinking: "It must be hard to live this way." I felt guilty as I pictured my condo back home, the luxuries I enjoyed daily, the abundance of food, clean and safe surroundings. But suddenly this thought came to my mind: *It is on streets like this that Jesus probably spends most of his time.*

This thought stopped me in my tracks, and it changed my view of global mission. The Christian experience I knew back in the States was abnormal from God's perspective. God sees wealthy and compartmentalized Christianity for what it is, so conveniently separated from the realities of most of the world, even from the realities of most Christian believers. Here I was for those 10 days, a welcome participant in a local congregation of 14 people making a shockingly outsized impact for the Kingdom of God. They were 14 people changing the lives of 60 families right in their own backyard! It was the first time I had caught a glimpse of the church Jesus referred to at Caesarea Philippi when he said in Matthew 16:18, "*The gates of hell will not prevail against it.*"

For the first time, I saw that church clearly in the mission of "*La Transfiguración*" to their community. Their first thought was not, "How do we grow our own church? They did not invest in an evangelism outreach program or subscribe to a marketing service to grow their internal numbers. Instead, they simply moved to impact the world that was right outside their door. The name of their congregation fit perfectly with what they were trying to do. They were making a "transfiguration". Meanwhile, back home, my "mid-sized" congregation of 1500 was trying to figure out how the other churches in town were pushing 2500 and how we could imitate what they were doing to also get there. The contrast between these two mindsets and worldviews set me back on my heels.

Understanding Kingdom Impact Jesus' Way

Vision is all about what you see. So, when you cast vision effectively you are giving people a picture of a possible future. The problem with the future is that it is always in motion! Just ask Yoda, who first made that assertion. But in terms of leading a congregation, that is not too far off the mark, nor is that the only piece of Star Wars memorabilia that has made its way into my tool kit. I am not above using a Yoda-ism to help engage with our culture.

However, the problem is when we let the values of our culture invade the mission. To a great extent, the church growth movement has done just that. "Bigger is better" is one of the doctrinal statements of corporate America. Today, it is akin to a doctrinal statement in many churches as well. When we think about growing the church, we understand this to mean getting more people into the pews. That goal is not wrong-spirited. All of us who are leading churches want to have more members of the Body of Christ present on Sundays, expressing their love for Jesus, growing in his Word, and helping to disciple one another. But for me and many of others who lead churches, the drive to see more people in the pews can become discouraging, defeating, and even unhealthy, especially if the idea of growing a large church has become an idol and a source of envy.

Paul wrote about this in his letter to the Philippians: *"It is true that some preach Christ out of envy and rivalry, but others out of goodwill. ¹⁶ The latter do so out of love, knowing that I am put here for the defense of the gospel.* ¹⁷ *The former preach Christ out of selfish ambition, not sincerely, supposing that they can stir up trouble for me while I am in chains.* ¹⁸ *But what does it matter? The important thing is that in every way, whether from false motives or true, Christ is preached. And because of this I rejoice" (Philippians 1: 15 – 18a).*

I know that, at times, I have preached Christ out of envy and rivalry. I have looked with envy at other churches in town that were, for whatever reason, more attractional, seemed more popular, or had more resources at their disposal (both human and financial). This can happen especially when, from a sinful base, I am making ministry about me. But the converse is also true. I have also preached Christ out of love. And when I do, I am in the place God wants me to be. All of us should be happy to see any Christ-centered and Bible-believing church grow, for we are on the same team. They are part of me, and I am part of them. Paul said as much in the passage quoted above.

Here is where a focus on Kingdom Impact can help with all the self-defeating tendencies associated with just working to grow your church. Growth strategies often result in just getting more spectators. There are churches today that are filled with people who mostly watch religious professionals worship, whether that is a worship leader, an inspirational pastor presenting the message, or the amazing vocalist delivering her solo. If the goal is just inspiration, we can employ many methods to create the atmosphere and excitement that will sustain a crowd. Entertainers and the owners of sports teams have the same goal — fill the seats! But Christian ministry should be different. We should be creating ministers and missionaries, not spectators. Missionaries often go out in twos and threes. Ministry most often happens in the small context and in the small moments. When Jesus talked about the Kingdom he came to establish, his emphasis was more often on the small scale, a seed, a coin, something lost, something found, or something discovered...

Not only does Kingdom Impact direct leaders away from trying to replicate the weekend worship experiences of larger and better-resourced churches, realizing that impact focuses on what happens *between* Sunday mornings. I have often told my congregation that the majority of the Kingdom Impact of our church does not happen during the set hour of worship or during planned and programmed midweek Bible studies and classes. Even on Sunday mornings, the majority of Kingdom work happens in the hallway, in the lobby, or narthex, on the couches in private conversations, and on the way to and from the sanctuary.

Most of the Kingdom Impact of the Body of Christ is *non-*professional, carried out by Jesus-followers who respond in the moment to situations of care, requests for prayer, providing support, love and answers, corrections and convictions, or are simply willing to just "be with" one another as conduits for the work of the Spirit. *That is just on Sunday.* All that spiritual caregiving is practice for the real Kingdom Impact that will begin on Monday when the members of the Body of Christ are released into the world. How many of us pay as much attention to the ministry done by our congregational members during the week as we do to counting worship attendance and offering on the weekend? Where do you perceive that the mission of Jesus is more alive and active? Now we are starting to see what Kingdom Impact means.

And here is the good news, even the best news. If your goal is Kingdom Impact rather than just growing your church, you already have everyone you need! You do not need a bigger membership to do it. *Kingdom Impact values the people you already have.* It values their gifts; it demonstrates gratitude for the resources already at hand. What it takes, however, is getting the focus off putting people *into* the pews, and instead, getting them *out* of the pews and *into* God's plan for reaching their friends, neighbors, and coworkers with the Gospel of Jesus Christ. No matter what size of church, you already have everyone you need to do this. What God needs now is for you to understand the call to lead your people to make Kingdom Impact *Jesus' way.*

In Matthew 13, Jesus presented six teaching stories to reveal important aspects of the Kingdom he came to establish in the world. This Kingdom is very different from anything the world has ever seen before. The power of Jesus' Kingdom parables is that they present compelling and memorable *pictures* of the Kingdom of God in action. What is the church supposed to look like? What is the church supposed to be doing? Jesus answered this question six different ways, and each one begins with the phrase: "The kingdom of heaven is like…" For you and I who are Jesus' followers today, these Kingdom parables offer essential instructions for how to make Kingdom Impact Jesus' Way — and claim that impact right on our corner.

Discussion Questions:

1. When have you felt as though weekend worship was like putting on a show?
2. How many people in your congregation respond more like spectators than missionaries? Why do you think they behave that way?
3. Have you ever ministered out of a mindset of envy?
4. How do you know when you are preaching Christ out of love?
5. Make a mental list of the key missionaries in your church, the gifts they bring and the ministries they are helping to lead. Where do you see that you already have everyone you need to begin to make Kingdom Impact in your local area?
6. What is at stake for you in the shift from Church Growth to the goal of Kingdom Impact?
7. What did you find interesting, challenging, or compelling about the story of Transfiguration Lutheran Church in Azul, Argentina?

CHAPTER 1

The Parable of the Sower —
Finding Good Soil and Planting There

"That same day Jesus went out of the house and sat by the lake. ² Such large crowds gathered around him that he got into a boat and sat in it, while all the people stood on the shore. ³ Then he told them many things in parables, saying: "A farmer went out to sow his seed. ⁴ As he was scattering the seed, some fell along the path, and the birds came and ate it up. ⁵ Some fell on rocky places, where it did not have much soil. It sprang up quickly, because the soil was shallow. ⁶ But when the sun came up, the plants were scorched, and they withered because they had no root. ⁷ Other seed fell among thorns, which grew up and choked the plants. ⁸ Still other seed fell on good soil, where it produced a crop—a hundred, sixty or thirty times what was sown. ⁹ Whoever has ears, let them hear."

Matthew 13: 1 – 9

This Kingdom parable takes us back into a common farming method in the ancient Near East. It is a method called "broadcasting". Farmers would walk their fields with satchels of seed at their sides. Grabbing a handful of seeds, they would make a broad, arcing motion, broadcasting the seeds over a wide area of cultivated ground.

So often when we read this parable we figuratively get "caught in the weeds" and think Jesus is concerned primarily with the seeds that do not grow, the ones that landed among the rocks and thorns. I know that I, and many of my pastor colleagues, get caught sermonizing on all the ways that we should all try harder to be good soil, rather than rocky, weedy, or *path-y* soil in the story. We imagine that if we just tried hard enough to be good soil, we could choke out the weeds before they choke us; we could dig out the rocks in our lives that keep us from growing deep; and we could chase away the birds before they eat us alive! Of course, like good cultural Westerners, we imagine ourselves as the stars of the parable: the seeds, who must prove themselves in a competitive world. In this way, we make the story about us rather than about God. News flash: we are not the stars of this story.

Here is the key piece of information we are forgetting — the farmer never intended for the seeds to grow along the path, or in the rocks, or in the weeds. That is not how farmers work. The parable is not about where the farmer did not intend the seed to go, where he over-broadcasted, it is about where the seeds were meant to go — into the soil of the field that the farmer prepared, the good soil, from which he intends to gain a harvest.

That changes the story completely! This is not a do-better story, or a work-harder, story. The star of the story is the Word of God, the Seed, making it into the environment the farmer had prepared for it. The side stories: the rocks, the weeds, and the path, are just to emphasize all the things that the good soil is not.

So where is that good soil? The good soil is where the farmer, God, has prepared it in advance. It is where he has plowed and churned up the hard crust, removing the rocks and the weeds. All that work was done in advance, not on the day of the sowing. Any farmer will warn you not to sow expensive seed in ground that is not prepared.

Here is the thing: there is good soil in every human heart, in the places primed for spiritual growth; often it is where people have deep questions, deep hurts and needs, and where the Spirit of God has been doing his loving work. Now, there are also places in our hearts where we feel self-assured, where we are self-satisfied with commitments to big rocks such as career, hobbies, and misplaced commitments to wealth, big houses, fancy cars, gadgets, etc. These things compete with or repel God's seed, they choke it out; or the seed itself is stolen by the winged enemy as Jesus later explained. In each of the bad soil conditions, the seeds cannot germinate. They will not grow for all the reasons Jesus mentioned. But in the good soil, where the ground has been prepared, the Gospel, the Seed, the Word of God will take root, grow, and produce fruit, fruit that multiplies many, many times. So, the goal is to find the good soil and sow in that place. Sowing the seed anywhere else is akin to "over-broadcasting", wasting time and resources.

So, what does this parable say to the Church — and to individual Christians — about greater Kingdom Impact? Answer: The seed is meant for the cultivated field. What the Church needs to be doing today is seeking the places in peoples' lives and in the community that are *already* receptive to the Word. Look for the plowed field; that is where you put seeds. It is where the soil has been turned over, churned up, and broken open. It is ready and receptive.

In a previous congregation I served, there was a man who grew to be a leader in the church, using his professional skills to help us better organize and administrate effectively. I will refer to him as Mike. Prior to being part of our church, Mike had a nominal Christian experience; but he grew dramatically in the Lord as he became involved in leadership, especially when he found that his professional gifts could be used to serve God. But Mike surprised me one day with a question that opened one of the deepest points of spiritual insecurity in his life. From the outside Mike appeared successful and confident in every way. He and his wife had a loving and supportive marriage; he had wonderful kids, all super-achievers; he and his family enjoyed a comfortable lifestyle in one of the better neighborhoods in our city. Let us say that Mike had everything this world could give to a person.

But at the root all that was a gnawing doubt and a deep-seated fear. Mike's big break professionally had come with the acquisition of a multi-million-dollar contract. His success with that client transformed his career almost overnight, moving him to the top. But something inside Mike caused him to react to this success with a feeling of shame. He feared that God was not behind it, in fact, he attributed this worldly success to the spiritual enemy, perhaps because with wealth had also come material temptations. Mike told me he feared that Satan had given him this advancement and that now he was on the devil's plan for his life rather than God's. I struggled for a few moments to know how to react Mike's fear. I knew the seriousness of the moment. He was trusting me with a place of insecurity and doubt that called almost all of his life, and all of the opportunities that his career provided for him and his family, into question. Inside, Mike feared the source was evil. I knew I needed to help Mike bring this fear into the light of God and plant the seed of God's Word in the right place so that it could grow.

Not knowing many of the details, I spoke carefully, asking Mike to consider God's power versus the power of the enemy. I asked him to consider all the good that had come from his promotions, the people he had been able to help with the resources that were available to him. Did that point to Satan's purposes or to God's? I also encouraged him to see how God was now using him as a leader in our church. I presented the evidence that this was God's grace at work in his life and that he might receive all this as a gift and continue to use it for God's work. Even if he had not done so, Mike could deliver all his successes into God's hands, returning them for use in Kingdom purposes.

In hindsight, I know I did not ask all the questions that I should have in that critical pastoral care moment. Had Mike done something with his success and power that made him feel guilty? Now, because I have more experience, I would ask that question and more. But I know that Mike left that day with less of a weight on his shoulders and less of a shadow over his self-perception and his relationship with God. Regardless of what had been the past, Mike saw that the future could always be placed in God's hands according to his grace. All that happened because a man uncovered the good soil in his life, the place of pain and confusion, the place torn open, where the Good News of Jesus could be planted. This is an example of good soil being revealed in an individual person.

But good soil can also be identified in a community. Finding it can open long-term places of missional investment and impact for a congregation. A few years into ministry at my current congregation, there were obvious signs that the church was not growing in key areas. While the original founding families included children and youth, some of them had graduated, others had moved away, and now there were the tell-tale signs of a dwindling children's ministry. I feared where this would lead. We had to reach new families. It felt like the clock was ticking, so I began to knock on doors in the neighborhoods around our church. I got the predictable results in a mid-sized, Midwestern city: many nice, smiling faces, lots of encouraging comments, but mostly the: "Thank you, I already have a church," dismissal. Fair enough, they did not need a second church. People should not need one of those anyways! I tried three neighborhoods, all with similar results.

Then, one day, I was driving on a main road, about a mile north of our church building. I passed a neighborhood I had not investigated. There were a few RV's and campers next to the road, and behind them, a series of mobile homes. Having already passed the road that led into the community, I turned around and proceeded to drive into a large neighborhood, comprising eight blocks, and about 100 homes! After three years of ministry in that town, I had completely overlooked this neighborhood. I felt increasingly embarrassed of my ignorance as I drove along the streets and witnessed children playing everywhere. Children, youth, and young families...

I set out into this neighborhood the very next week, not fully appreciating at first what God was doing. Door after door opened to me; smiling faces invited me in; I enjoyed twenty-minute conversations leaning on porch railings. Then I would ask my favorite question for door-to-door evangelism: "So, do you have a church that you go to?" The answer I got from many of the people was this: "No, I don't have a church, but I would love to have one." After a few experiences like this I began to respond, "We would *love* to be that church!"

This began a five-year adventure in which our congregation invested in that neighborhood. We helped some residents repair their homes, we helped others who were unemployed with groceries or gift cards, and we started inviting the families to church events. But that was where we met with our first setback. These folks were very receptive to knocks on the door, help with their homes, and offers of prayer. But coming to church? For some reason that was a barrier. Perhaps for some, they imagined that 'church people' had it all together. That can be intimidating. But we kept at it, even though targeted events failed to attract the residents of this neighborhood. Finally, we got the message that this was a situation where the church needed to be *fully* missional, to go into the world, rather than to ask the world to come to us. We started dreaming of a community-based youth ministry offered right in the neighborhood, perhaps an outdoor summer program.

That was when the next door opened. We got a call from the property manager in the mobile home park. She said: "We have a little office on site that we are trying to rent. It seems like your church is really doing some positive things in our neighborhood. Could we offer you a place to work right here?" There are times when

God just drops things right in your lap. This was one of them. The manager was a Christian and understood the benefit of a church adopting a neighborhood. She opened the door for just such an opportunity.

Quickly we pulled together a team of neighborhood parents with whom we had built relationships, and we met together at a local restaurant. The simple question we asked was: "If we rented this space, what should it be used for? What do you think families like yours need?" Two clear answers were arrived at: first, a place for kids to do homework after school that had computers and internet access; second, a place where kids could gather safely with trusted adult supervision for positive interactions and spiritual support. Jacob's Well ministry was born out of those requests.

Imagine a church opening a little storefront ministry only one mile from their location. Seems absurd right? But it is not absurd when you understand the context, not when you have really discerned the location of the good soil that God has prepared. Jacob's Well began as a place for after school tutoring, staffed by volunteers from our congregation. We partnered with a local food shelf to provide snacks and beverages. A young schoolteacher made Jacob's Well his personal mission. He served as the program leader and developer of the ministry. He created a workable plan, and suddenly we had a community-based youth ministry that was <u>larger</u> than the youth ministry we had at our church's main building. We started offering Friday night events that gathered more kids, and slowly we helped this group of students intermingle with youth from the church. But the key moment happened that first summer. Boldly, we moved all our midweek children's and youth ministry from the church <u>to</u> Jacob's Well, offering a Wednesday night Bible club at the playground of the mobile home park. The kickoff event was a BBQ night with inflatable games. We had seventy people in attendance that first evening. A huge outreach for our little church.

I will never forget walking around that night, watching

Jacob's Well ministry begin to integrate into the larger life of our congregation. Friendships started to form; new leaders were identified; and plans began for a community garden (Jacob's Garden), further cementing the sense that our congregation had truly moved into the neighborhood.

As the next school year began, the youth from Jacob's Well started to show up at church on Sundays and on Wednesday nights all by themselves. Many of those kids walked or rode their bikes, clearly showing that they valued being part of a congregation that demonstrated care, a church that was learning to plant in the right place at the right time — in the good soil. That year we saw that our children's and youth ministry triple in their impact. This was not without growing pains of course. Thirty kids from unchurched backgrounds suddenly walking through the doors without their parents was enough to thoroughly shake up a middle-class congregation. But I watched as the members learned to love as Jesus loves. Deep down we knew we had discovered part of Jesus' mission that had been hidden from our view for years.

Missionaries always start their mission where their gifts and passions intersect with the world's greatest needs. It is this corner they claim. If the community they are looking to serve lacks child-care, as was the case in Azul, Argentina, a church of fourteen individuals can meet that need and produce a great harvest. If a Midwestern church finds a community with needs for spiritual and educational support for children, the church can meet that need with intentional investment. It all begins with discerning the good soil, and discernment, of course, is fueled by prayer. We will not see the good soil available in our community, or in the life of the person with a pastoral care need, without the gift of God's discernment and constant conversation with him. He must show the need to us first and then call us to meet it. When we start to see the world through Jesus' eyes, we start looking for the *directions* to the field God has prepared in the people we meet every day.

That is the first principle that we can take from Jesus' Matthew 13 parables, the first Kingdom instruction from Jesus for greater Kingdom Impact. Plant where there is good soil, often where pain or stress have opened up the ground. Stay and cultivate, and look for the harvest. Do not get caught up in the weeds, rocks, and thorns. The seed is not going to grow there anyway! Congregations who seek to make Kingdom Impact, look for the place where God is already working and seek to just join in.

Kingdom Impact Example, Sowing in the Good Soil: Bethany Baptist Church, Peoria IL — A Ministry to Adopting and Fostering Families.

Bethany Baptist Church in Peoria, Illinois, became involved in supporting adopting and fostering families in 2005. There was already a group of families in the congregation actively involved in fostering children when Pastor Daniel Bennett (formally the Youth Pastor) became the Family Pastor. He and other leaders felt God's call to support these families in a much more intentional way, partnering congregational resources with the domestic resources these parents were already employing along with monthly support from the State of Illinois' programs. Bethany's effort to make this a more robust and multifaceted ministry grew from the awareness of the challenges these families face, and the desire to see the Body of Christ support them with spiritual and financial resources.

Beyond this, the leaders at Bethany wanted to build into the congregation a Biblical and theological understanding of God's call to love and care for those without consistent parental figures. They also wanted to plant the power of God's Word into the good soil of families who were faithfully receiving children by adoption or into foster care. This passion to bring Christian mission into the realities and challenges faced by both adopting and fostering parents, makes this example an ideal one for the case of sowing in good soil. Bethany wanted to make sure that the hope found in Jesus Christ found its way to those children, but also to the parents seeking to support them, in practical and powerful ways. Over time, the ministry came to be called "Open Hearts, Open Homes". (For a more detailed account of the ministry, check out Pastor Bennett's book, *A Passion for the Fatherless, Developing a God-Centered Ministry to Orphans,* by Pastor Daniel J. Bennett, published in 2014).

When many of us think about the choice of adoption we often imagine the obvious challenges faced by both the adopting family and the adopted child. There are so many uncertainties about the future. How will this child adapt to our family and culture, especially if they have come from a very different set of cultural values, or from an orphanage in a country in Eastern Europe or from a poorer part of Asia, as many adopted children do? Families and adoption agencies, both here and abroad, spend months or years to make sure children are matched with an appropriate family who can care for them and provide that better future for which they are hoping. In the case where adopted children are infants, the uncertainties are even higher as adopting parents may not know what kinds of physical or emotional trauma their adopted child might have been through. In the case of international adoptions, often these details are obscured or not available. Families that choose adoption have weighed those risks; they understand that the good they seek to do, either in completing their sense of call to parenthood, or in rescuing a child from less desirable conditions, outweighs the uncertainties. A huge amount of faith and trust in God is always part of the equation. Adoption is certainly a calling that God places upon the hearts of special parents, especially for those who want to help others choose against aborting a pregnancy.

An equally challenging and rewarding call for a family is to foster children from within their own country, working with local and national agencies to provide a safe place for children who had to be removed from their natural parents either temporarily or permanently. Inherent to being foster parents, is the fact that you will have these children for a limited and unknown amount of time. The ability to let go of them when the time comes might be as hard as the difficulties faced in being a surrogate parent from day to day.

Here is a summary description of how Bethany's ministry, Open Hearts Open Homes, functions as it seeks to plant good seed in the good soil of those choosing to adopt or foster.

First, Open Hearts Open Homes establishes a clear Biblical foundation for why the local church should have compassion for the disenfranchised, the orphan or 'fatherless' child:

a. God is a compassionate God, (Ex. 33:19).
b. Orphans are one of the groups that receive God's special compassion, (Ex. 22:21–27; Deuteronomy 10:18a; Ps. 10:14b; 68:5; Hos. 14:3).
c. God's people are to have compassion for the orphan, (Isa. 1:17; James 1:27).

The ministry leaders came to this beautiful vision for a congregationally-based ministry to the fatherless and those who love them:

1. The orphan needs the church where he or she may discover the unconditional love of the Heavenly Father.
2. The Church needs the orphan to remind us that all of us are orphaned by the reality of sin and that God has chosen to adopt us through Jesus Christ.
3. And finally, the orphan advocate (the adopting and fostering family) needs the Church. The call to adoption or fostering is not one that can be accomplished by one family on their own. It must be a community effort of God's people.

Upon this Biblical foundation, Bethany sought to surround these families with a Gospel-centered community. The ministry of Open Hearts Open Homes is extremely broad, seeking to support not only those families who already have adopted or fostered a child, but those who are feeling God's call to do so. But beyond that, they committed to educate the entire congregation on the Biblical foundation for serving the fatherless and serving those who are serving them. The goal was to create a culture of adoption awareness so that children who entered the congregation this way were loved on every level.

Here are some of the specific services and initiatives by which Bethany Baptist equips and supports these families:

Families that are seeking to adopt / foster, or are already doing so, are approved for participating in the Adoption Fund which can help them afford the costs. These costs can range from $10,000 to $45,000 or more, depending upon the type of adoption process they are using: private, agency, domestic or international. To qualify, these families must participate in an Orphan Care Bible Study, complete an application, go through an interview process, and finally, be recommended for financial support by Bethany's elder board. This fund is supported by individuals and families of Bethany as well as grants through Lifesong for Orphans, a Christian organization in Illinois that supports churches with adoption ministries.

Once approved, these families receive prayer, financial support, ongoing Biblical counselling, participation in a support group with other adopting/fostering families, and help with physical needs such as meals, transportation, clothing, and opportunities for childcare provided through the church. Simply put, these families are mentored and supported in every way as they travel the journey of opening their home to the 'fatherless' child, of which there are roughly 100 million worldwide.

Parallel ministries have developed at Bethany that only contribute to this robust, congregational call to compassion. Annual mission trips are offered to visit international orphanages. Members of the church are invited to become part of the Open Hearts Open Homes support teams which provide the material and financial supports listed above. A ministry called Safe Families was also introduced to

Bethany. Families that are not able to go the full route of adoption or fostering, may open their homes for short periods of time to children from families that are experiencing short-term financial or emotional stress. The goal is to get ahead of situations that, if allowed to continue, might result in state agencies being called in due to neglect or abuse. Safe Families receives child referrals from social workers, schools, hospitals, and other sources. Bethany families that participate in Safe Families are trained and go through a background check so that they may receive a child or children from a family in crisis for just a few days or up to a year, allowing the parents receive counseling or other assistance to get them back to a place of stability. Once life is normalized, these children are reunited with their parents. Members of Bethany may also donate furniture and other essentials that can be used by families who are sheltering local children.

All in all, the goal of Open Hearts Open Homes is to mobilize the Bethany congregation to be a safe, equipped, and welcoming congregation for children from all over the country and all over the world. All this is done so that they will experience the love of Jesus right at the point of their most critical need, to be fathered and cared for by the people of God. This ministry is a wonderful example of a congregation carefully sowing the seed of God's Word into good soil that was prepared in advance. In these kinds of situations, the Word of God flourishes as the grace of Jesus Christ is applied where it is so desperately needed. The ministry of Bethany Baptist to children and parents is well-known locally, and has inspired many families in the area to open their hearts to adoption and foster care.

Pastor Daniel Bennett said this: "The elders were unanimously excited about being obedient to God in this area as they saw how his Word is passionate about this ministry." (Bennett, A Passion for the Fatherless).

Discussion Questions:

1. Most often, when we imagine how God's Word is used in a local congregation, we think of the sermon on Sunday, midweek Bible studies, or small groups. How did you react to the story of Bethany Baptist's plan to inspire and equip an entire congregation to understand and participate in a specific mission to their community?

2. How do you respond to this view of the parable of the sower, seeing it as a directive to identify good soil in our communities, or specific areas in people's lives, that are uniquely prepared and receptive?

3. The leaders of Bethany Baptist saw in the Word of God the obvious call to have compassion for others. When you consider the community around your church, what comes to mind as a place or circumstance where the power of God's Word and Christian compassion could make a difference?

4. Come up with three ideas where you or your congregation are uniquely positioned to sow in the good soil around you.

5. Now look at your congregation as it currently is. What gifts or resources are waiting to be used to meet the needs you have just identified?

6. What is the next step you could take?

CHAPTER 2

The Parable of the Weeds —
Confronting Evil on the Ground

"Jesus told them another parable: "The kingdom of heaven is like a man who sowed good seed in his field.
25 But while everyone was sleeping, his enemy came and sowed weeds among the wheat, and went away.
26 When the wheat sprouted and formed heads, then the weeds also appeared.

27 "The owner's servants came to him and said, 'Sir, didn't you sow good seed in your field? Where then did the weeds come from?'

28 "'An enemy did this,' he replied.

"The servants asked him, 'Do you want us to go and pull them up?'

²⁹ "'No,' he answered, 'because while you are pulling the weeds, you may uproot the wheat with them. ³⁰ Let both grow together until the harvest. At that time I will tell the harvesters: First collect the weeds and tie them in bundles to be burned; then gather the wheat and bring it into my barn.'"

Matthew 13: 24 – 30

The reality of evil is one of the reasons why some people struggle to believe that a good and loving God created the world and continues to sustain it. The world does not appear to be working right. Things seem broken, or at least not ideal, perfect, just, right, or satisfying, for all. We feel that on the macro level, but more personally on the micro level. Recent events have put an exclamation mark on all of that: the global pandemic, increasing economic disparity, deep racial and political divides, as well as unpredictable weather.

The common observation is: "If there is a good and powerful God, that God should do a better job of confronting evil." Some even suggest that the very fact of evil itself is proof that God does not exist, at least not the loving and powerful God revealed in the Bible. The common dilemma presented is that God must be good, but not powerful; or that God must be powerful, but not good. Often this idea is posited as a faith crisis. But let us be clear: it is a false crisis because this is a false dichotomy. This faith crisis comes from the perspective that if there is a God, he should be controlling all things down to the minute details and therefore responsible for everything that takes place. But that is not the way the Bible reveals the role God has chosen for himself in creation, including his relationship with evil, not if you study the entire Bible and understand how Scripture balances and interprets itself.

Instead, we find a much more compelling reality put forth in Scripture. God created human beings as his representatives on earth to do his will. God seeks the freedom of human beings to respond to him, to act and to partner with him according to his invitation. The creation story in Genesis, chapter 2, presents Adam and Eve as caretakers, serving God and his will for the world. And yet, it is in the same creation story that we witness the Fall of humanity into sin. We see clearly in Genesis chapter 3 – 5, a 'snowballing' of human sin beginning in the Garden of Eden. That snowball effect has continued, and human choices are responsible for much of the evil we see today. The effect of sin has been that human nature is fundamentally oriented in selfish and sinful rebellion against God's nature and his good intention. Each of us have a "dominion" like that which God gave to Adam and Eve in the Garden. We have dominion in our thoughts, words, and actions. We are also accountable for them before God, according to his law.

But that is only part of the story. In the Parable of The Wheat and The Weeds, Jesus goes further to explain the origin of evil. Evil was *sown* into creation and into the human heart. But *who* did that, and *what* initiated it? Genesis records this in the story of Adam's and Eve's fall from grace through the influence of the serpent, but Jesus gives us another picture in this parable to help us understand even more. Once again, as in the Parable of The Sower and the Seed, God is pictured as a farmer who has carefully set aside a field and planted his seed. Again, this seed can be understood as God's Word, his intention, his expression. But, according to the parable, an enemy came at night with weed seeds, and sowed them in the field to disrupt the harvest. We see here the Fall of humanity, as described in Genesis 3, using a different metaphor.

Let us back up to the previous parable. There, the farmer sowed seed in the good soil, expecting a harvest. The seed fell elsewhere too, but the harvest was expected from the field, not from among the rocks, the thorns, or the path. The goal is the *harvest*; the farmer will return to the field to seek it at the right time. So, who would want to disrupt the farmer's harvest, to hurt him, to contradict his efforts, to undermine his purposes, to steal what was to be the farmer's alone, and to spoil his crop? Who is that enemy who is actively seeking, on the most basic level, to destroy God's intentions for creation? This enemy is also our spiritual enemy, who seeks to disrupt our earthly and our spiritual lives, and to prevent you and me from being part of the harvest. That enemy is Satan. Jesus plainly tells his disciples this in his explanation of the parable:

> *"He answered, "The one who sowed the good seed is the Son of Man. ³⁸ The field is the world, and the good seed stands for the people of the kingdom. The weeds are the people of the evil one, ³⁹ and the enemy who sows them is the devil. The harvest is the end of the age, and the harvesters are angels" (Matthew 13: 37 – 39).*

Where weeds grow, crops die. Weeds take the resources of water and nutrients; weeds take space. In the previous parable about the good soil, Jesus told us that where there are weeds already growing, the good seed will be choked out. This is the clearest teaching in the New Testament about the reality and nature of evil. Jesus addresses the origin of evil, but also, important to the false dichotomy we described a moment ago, Jesus explains how the fact of evil in the world is <u>not</u> mutually exclusive with a good, loving, *and* all-powerful God. Jesus also tells us plainly in this parable the reason why our good God has not simply removed evil from the world. God has delayed his judgment — the pulling up of the weeds — because some wheat would be destroyed in the process.

And here is where each of us are required to be honest with one another and ourselves. Evil has been sown into our hearts too. Weeds are growing here, in me. If God applied the weed killer today, I would not survive. Would you? Therefore, from this parable we understand that an evil kingdom is growing alongside the good Kingdom of God.

Here is the key to understanding the parable: *both* kingdoms are increasing. The Kingdom of God and the counter-kingdom of God's enemy are both growing and increasing at the same time and in the same location.

The case can be made that where the Gospel has been planted and is growing, opportunity and the quality of life for many has measurably improved. The case can also be made that where the Gospel has not been planted, opportunity, quality of life, and many other factors, have not improved in the same way, or have even gone backward for many people. Now this is too general. We must be honest that, in many cases, imperfect people who planted the Gospel also did harm to those who were receiving it. The Kingdom of God on earth, as it has been built by human beings, is rife with mistakes, sinful actions, unfortunate and devastating events. The story of colonialism around the world is one of divided intentions. While Christian missionaries and ministers brought God's Word, in the mix was also the motivation of greed for wealth and territory by the very countries that sent and supported those missionaries. But in that mixed field, God was able to work his purposes as well. The wheat and the weeds are always in the mix whenever human beings are involved — the work of God and the influence of sin. It is also very difficult to separate the two in the lives of people, as Jesus makes so abundantly clear in this parable. Even the angels would get it wrong!

All that is true on the macro level, but it is also true on the micro level in my own life. God's good purposes are on the increase in the parts of my life where his seed is growing. In the parts of my life that are not yet fully submitted to God, evil is at work and growing. For that to stop, evil must be confronted where it grows! That is how we can apply this parable to understand Jesus' mandate to the church on the ground today, on the very corner where your church is planted. The Church must actively confront evil in our day.

But first, let us review. Jesus shows us here that these two realities, the Kingdom of God, and the kingdom of evil, are in tension and in competition on the ground, and will remain as such until the harvest. God's judgement will fall upon evil at the end of time — at the harvest. God's harvest will take place regardless of the incursion of evil through the works of man or through the work of our spiritual enemy. At the harvest, evil will be finally rooted out and judged (burned).

That is why we have this prerogative to preach the Gospel and to do Gospel work, partnering with God to renew this world in the image of his Son. We are called to bring others into relationship with God through Jesus Christ now, before the judgment, before the weed killer is put down. God has delayed his judgment for the preservation of the wheat, to preserve its harvest, but also so that a "sorting out" can occur at the right time on the ground level regarding who, and what, are the weeds, and who and what are the wheat.

This brings us to the role of the local church on the ground. We are not the judge or the harvester, but we have the responsibility to confront the effect of the weeds in God's field. We must confront evil in the world and evil in ourselves. We must be as relentless in one as we are in the other.

There is a great tradition of the Church confronting evil in previous centuries. Christians confronted homelessness and hunger through urban missions, disease, and other health concerns through the establishment of hospitals. Christians moved to abolish slavery. They worked against the negative effects of alcohol through temperance movements and modern substance abuse recovery programs and ministries. In previous centuries, Christians led the way in creating protections for workers and children from exploitation in the workplace, confronting communism and other authoritarian political movements on the left and the right. Today the Church is working to confront the evils of on-demand abortion, and to help our culture face the continued impact of racism, both here and in other parts of the world. All this and more is the work of the Church on the ground as part of the mission of God.

When Christians engage in this kind of Kingdom-action it is a strong and positive witness to those who do not yet know Jesus. When secular people see Christians confront what they also categorize as evil, there is an attraction to Jesus Christ like no other. Remember, people who do not yet know the Lord were still created in God's image. They too can judge when something is wrong.

A great example of Kingdom Impact from the 19th Century

occurred during the period of "Indian removal" to reservation lands. Moravian missionaries had been working amongst the Cherokee people in the American southeast, establishing churches and schools. The Gospel was making strong inroads in the Cherokee nation. But then President Andrew Jackson took extraordinary efforts to force the Cherokee people out of their homelands to make way for white settlers. Against the order of the Supreme Court, Jackson had the army forcibly remove the Cherokee, making them walk a thousand miles to eastern Oklahoma. The Moravians responded in peaceful and righteous Christian protest. Some went ahead to Oklahoma to set up a mission to receive the people they loved, again building a school and a church. Other Moravians felt the call to walk the trail with the Cherokee families, powerfully demonstrating the call of Christ to identify with those who are suffering. This is a very clear example of the wheat and the weeds growing together. The efforts of the administration of President Jackson to remove the tribes of the southeastern United States did not prevent the Moravian missionaries from faithfully witnessing the true nature of Jesus Christ to the Cherokee people.

Another good example of Christians confronting evil was the stand taken by Lutheran pastors confronting fascism in Europe during the Second World War. In a former congregation where I served, there was a wonderfully wise, older lady who had been a student at the time of Hitler's Germany. Her pastor was part of Dietrich Bonhoeffer's resistance and he had a profound impact upon her and his other Confirmation students. Though he spent much of his time jailed by the Nazis, when he was free, he helped his students fill violin cases with food for each of them to carry into the Jewish ghetto. Who was going to suspect a fourteen-year-old girl going for music lessons? Following her pastor, she delivered food to those being marginalized and victimized by a government out of control.

The Parable of the Weeds gives us a clear mandate: congregations must be looking for ways to confront evil right on their corners, in their neighborhoods, cities, states, countries, and in the world. Part of our church life, even represented in our calendar of events, should be efforts aimed at confronting evil in the world and in ourselves.

I invite you to stop and take the next 15 – 20 minutes in quiet reflection and internet research on the realities of evil in your city or area. Using the space below, write down the biggest examples or manifestations of evil right where you live. Remember, you are trying to identify the "weeds". Next to the asterisk in the chart below, indicate one idea of how your congregation could confront this evil on the ground. Consider how, in many cases, that might mean partnering with ministries and agencies that are already confronting those problems. But make sure that you are also envisioning new ministries that could be born right from within your congregation.

> The Weeds I Can See Growing Around Me:

Now do the harder task: Identify five examples of weeds you see in yourself: attitudes, behaviors, idols, biases, and prejudices. Write them in the box below:

My guess is that you needed a break after doing that. It can be depressing and discouraging to look so critically at our own community and also at ourselves. Often it is in these places where we are most blind to the weeds that disrupt God's harvest. It is hard to be confronted with all these realities today, but here is precisely where the words of Jesus speak so powerfully. In this parable, the landowner says plainly, "'An enemy did this'" *(Matthew, 13: 28a).*

In a more personal way now, we can understand the angry response of the servants (the angels) in the parable: *"Do you want us to go and pull them up?" (Matthew 13: 28b).* I too have had that same righteous anger rise in me. Maybe you have prayed for God to bring his judgment now. But Jesus' answer is telling: *"'No,' he answered, 'because while you are pulling up the weeds, you may root up the wheat with them'" (Matthew 13: 29).* There can be no more definitive statement from God as to why evil persists and seems to be growing, and why God has not simply removed evil from the world as he is fully capable of doing. But here is the main point of the parable: The wheat is growing too and is in conflict with the weeds for space and resources. The battle is taking place on the ground. That means you and I are part of that battle.

One of the ways that I challenge my congregation is for each person to identify their Kingdom Cause. God will share his heart with us if we are listening and sensitive to what he is saying and what impressions he is giving. If we develop that inner ear, that spiritual ear, we will start to understand the things that wound the heart of God. When I meet with couples preparing to be married, I often ask them to think and pray about a shared Kingdom Cause that will become part of their mission in the world as a new Adam and Eve. My wife and I identified early on in our relationship a mutual concern for children in poverty. We have learned to focus our extra giving to Christian organizations in the world that are fighting on that front. Whatever your Kingdom Cause, God sees that evil too and wants to address it in creation as part of his renewing work in Christ through you. Since we are Jesus' hands and feet in the world,

God's renewing work happens when we connect with God's heart and take action for Kingdom Impact. So now consider this question: "What is/are my Kingdom Causes?" (Take some time to journal in the box below):

How am I connecting with the heart of God for the world? What is/are my Kingdom Cause(s)?

What scriptural support do I find for this concern?

How might I start to take action?

A husband and wife joined our church a few years back with many Kingdom Causes already planted in their hearts. The wife especially had a burden for those who have no voice or are caught in situations of despair and injustice through no fault of their own. Her husband too was drawn into this same calling. In a powerful way, the wife became the heart of this shared passion and the husband became the head. Together they became a powerful force in our congregation's mission outreaches, organizing to support the growing plight of international refugees. Together Tim and Gretchen dreamed up a refugee walk that has become an annual event each fall. Individuals and families sign up to walk on a specific day for the purpose of raising money for organizations *on the ground* around the world addressing the needs of refugees, providing refugee care kits for distribution to those who are currently living in refugee camps. Through Tim and Gretchen, our congregation got beyond the political rhetoric regarding refugees, to learn that there are upwards of 80 million people displaced from their own countries *(The United Nations High Commissioner for Refugees, July, 2020)*. We discovered that almost half of them are children, and that the average stay for a person in a refugee camp is seventeen years. We learned about the ministries of pastors serving churches in camps and how education and healthcare works in that environment. Both Voice of the Martyrs and International Justice Mission have provided important educational material to inform us.

Each year, as part of the refugee walk, Tim and Gretchen work hard to make the event more than just a fundraiser. Each walker is assigned the identity of a real displaced person in the world, complete with name, picture, and backstory. As we walk, we encounter presenters, and situations placed along the route, that bring to life the heart-wrenching decisions that refugees are forced to make every day of their journeys. It has been a life-changing experience for many in our congregation and for others in the community. This is just one of Tim's and Gretchen's shared Kingdom Causes.

Individual congregations, and individual Christians, must be engaged in the battle against evil in all its forms. It is part of how we realize Kingdom Impact in the world. But we also must remember that battle is also within. The weeds are in ourselves too. It is why we must resist the feeling of self-righteousness associated with pointing out evil in the world. We must never see other human beings as enemies. That is not the Kingdom response. This is a spiritual battle, not a physical or political one. Human beings are not the enemy, but rather captives and hostages in Satan's destructive plan. But we are here as Christ's representatives, to be part of his rescue. As Ephesians 6: 12 tells us, *"For our struggle is not against flesh and blood, but against the rulers, against the authorities, against the powers of this dark world and against the spiritual forces of evil in the heavenly realms" (Ephesians 6:12).*

Jesus tells us in this parable that God has delayed his judgment of evil for one simple and grace-filled reason: he wants as many people as possible to come out of the weeds. What is interesting about Jesus' choice of words is that the seed sown by the enemy of God is not just any kind of weed. It is a tall grass remarkably similar to wheat, called tares. Tares mimic the wheat in every way as they grow until the time of the harvest. But at the point of the harvest, the tares will not produce the head of new seed the farmer is looking to harvest.

If our goal is to rescue every potential wheat seed, we must treat every human being as a wheat, not as a weed. What appears to be a weed may in fact be wheat in disguise, or just so entangled that you cannot distinguish them correctly. If angels would struggle to identify wheat in each case, certainly we are incapable. So, God has given us the task of preaching the Gospel, to bring men and women lovingly out of the weeds and into the Kingdom, before the weed killer is applied at Jesus' return. Every human being is a friend of God waiting to happen. That is where the real battle is, to move a person to the wheat. But we must start with ourselves or we will be powerless to do it for another. So, we love and preach, preach and serve, serve and confront the evil of the counter-kingdom. That is our job. We leave the time of the harvest to God.

KINGDOM IMPACT EXAMPLE, FIGHTING THE WEEDS IN THE GROUND: ROANOKE MENNONITE CHURCH, ROANOKE, IL — REFUGEE RESETTLEMENT.

Few of us have escaped awareness of the plight of displaced people around the world. Today there are over 80 million world-wide today, easily more than there have ever been. In recent decades, conflict and food insecurity have seen refugee camps in Africa expand dramatically. Memorable, from the time of the most recent presidential campaigns in the United States in 2019 and 2020, was the march of desperate people from Central America northward, sparking both fear and compassion among many in the American church while further raising the level of vitriol in domestic political debates. In increasing numbers, many refugees have also made the desperate journey to leave northern Iraq and Syria after the rise of the Islamic State's brutal and inhumane regime. These refugees sought safety in Turkey and Europe sparking international outrage when it was discovered that many had paid their life savings to join overcrowded boats heading across the Mediterranean. Again, the politicization of these stories had the effect of distracting us from the plight of fellow human beings who had few options. (None of us will forget the image of the Syrian boy lying dead on the beach).

In the midst of all the political bluster and distraction, many Christians have discerned the opportunity for the Church to be a source of welcome and support for displaced people. Christians have a long history of providing this support. Particularly when displaced people come to our borders seeking help, there is the chance for churches in prosperous western democracies to witness quietly to the love of Jesus Christ, helping those who are true asylum seekers find a new start.

Following a rich history in human rights activism in their denomination, Roanoke Mennonite, in Roanoke, Illinois, felt the call to live out this compassionate heritage when they learned about the plight of Central Americans coming to the southern border of the United States. Some of their leaders became connected to a Mennonite church in San Antonio, Texas, that was fearlessly stepping into the gap when those who were admitted to the United States lawfully as asylum seekers, were bussed to San Antonio and, literally, dropped off, with no resources or support. Roanoke Mennonite was inspired by the work of this church to begin to look for ways to assist asylum seekers in Illinois.

Through a family connection in Arizona, Roanoke Mennonite leaders learned specifically about two Guatemalan siblings, Mayan by culture, who made this perilous journey for the promise of safety and opportunity in America. With the added difficulty that Spanish was not their first language (they spoke a Mayan dialect), they had been separated at the border while awaiting their asylum cases, which can be three to five years in length. Because the brother had disabilities, he was sent to a foster care ministry in Michigan that specialized in helping in these cases, while the sister, who was his caregiver, was routed to an ICE detention center in Arizona where she remained for five months. When Roanoke Mennonite agreed to sponsor both brother and sister through the asylum process, bus tickets were purchased to bring the sister to Illinois. The brother was transported by case workers from Michigan.

The sister's trip was particularly difficult as she was unable to understand English well enough to make the correct bus transfers. When the church pastors learned that she was on the wrong bus and was headed to Chicago in the middle of the first wave of the COVID-19 outbreak, they contacted the bus company and arranged to meet her in Davenport, Iowa. Soon after, they were able to reunite this family in crisis after nine months of separation in the system.

The approach that this church took to caring for the needs of their new friends in Christ demonstrates the greater role the church can play as a center of community organization. Rather than relying only on the human resources in their own congregation, the pastors quickly gathered professionals from around the area: a lawyer, social workers, a professor, both churched and unchurched people, all in the effort to help establish a support network for the Guatemalans. The church is paying for most of the costs to support them, and will continue to do so, until a final decision is made regarding their asylum cases. Hopefully, with their roots established in a loving community, this brother and sister may remain in the Roanoke area indefinitely. Someday they may even be established as American citizens with a powerful testimony of the generosity of American Christians.

Husband and wife pastors Bryan and Jolene Miller explained that it was not difficult to get their congregation to embrace the idea of refugee resettlement. Centuries ago, Mennonite Christians were persecuted, sometimes violently, and were often among those who had to become religious refugees, leaving their homes, and seeking a safe place to restart their lives. One of the places they found refuge was in the American Midwest where they were promised religious freedom. This experience in their own denominational history, has given many Mennonite churches a basic moral and spiritual calling to be the hands and feet of Christ, fighting injustice, human rights abuses, and the results of systemic evil which causes millions of people today to still seek refuge. Helping a set of siblings might not be the winning of this battle, but it reminds us of the 'starfish principle': while not all can be rescued and the world cannot be changed overnight, we do what we can to save the ones that are within our reach. While one church could never address all the questions or issues associated with immigration today, a single congregation can make a world of difference for one or two displaced people. When the effects of evil in our broken world are fought by Christians on the ground, that battle is usually one situation, and one life, at a time.

Since coming to Illinois, the lives of this sister and brother (who want to remain anonymous) are improving. The brother, who has Down Syndrome, is receiving therapy, education, and support for his condition; things that were unavailable to him in their community in Guatemala. The sister has a strong and present faith and attends worship via the internet (during the COVID-19 quarantine) with Roanoke Mennonite even though her English is minimal. Through translation offered by her community of support, she constantly expresses her thanks for how God guided and provided for her and her brother. As she now has many physical needs met, she has started to dream about the opportunities that may now be available for her in a new country. Though she had little education growing up, she is now receiving tutoring through the network of support at Roanoke Mennonite.

When a local congregation engages together in this kind of intensive ministry to individuals in crisis, God enacts growth for all who are involved. Pastor Jolene talked about how members of the church have gained a much greater awareness and sensitivity to the difficult path that asylum seekers face. It is very different to experience the plight of refugees directly and personally, as part of Christian outreach, as opposed to simply reading about it in the news and drawing your own conclusions. Even with a strong team of professional and well-resourced people involved, the process of working through the asylum application has still been frustrating and exhausting. Members of Roanoke Mennonite have realized that for those going through the process on their own, and without resources, it must be nearly impossible. Pastor Jolene expressed that the intensity of their conviction and commitment toward immigration reform has significantly increased.

As part of building the network of support, Roanoke Mennonite partnered with other Christian congregations, as well as individuals in the community who claimed no faith affiliation, and yet cared deeply about justice and oppression. Pastor Jolene said, "It has built a bridge between the church and these individuals and has helped to counter the secular perception of aloof and self-righteous Christians who offer lip-service but follow up with little to no tangible action. These individuals in the support team have even voiced the possibility that they will come and visit our congregation and could see themselves as becoming part of a church that does the things that we do. This is not an outcome we ever imagined!"

Within the congregation, the pastors have noticed that there has been an increase in concern and sensitivity toward those whose circumstances in life are hard. Their work with this family of asylum seekers has opened new conversations that facilitate compassion and education. Those actively involved have become more aware and sympathetic regarding the impact of trauma, and the long and far-reaching ways it affects individuals emotionally, psychologically, and in many other ways. This adds a whole new layer of compassion for those facing displacement due to violence, famine, and poverty. Pastor Jolene said, "Even now, months later, our work with this family is a deep source of encouragement and hope to me as I witness the love of Jesus making a profound impact right here where I live and serve."

Discussion Questions:

1. The story of Roanoke Mennonite's work with members of a refugee family demonstrates the ability of the local church to concentrate care and support to make a dramatic difference in the lives of just a few individuals. This is the "starfish" principle. When you consider your congregation, is there an issue like this where you may be able to concentrate the care of the people of God and make a difference in even one person's life?

2. Refer to the places in this chapter where you brainstormed ideas about confronting the effects of evil on the ground. Having had time for those ideas to clarify further, what might you bring to the leaders of your church as a way for your congregation to confront the "weeds" in your community.

3. Is there a personal Kingdom Cause that has begun to grab hold of your heart? If so, how might you commit today to research further and take action in order to do the work of the Kingdom and rescue more of God's field for the harvest?

4. When it comes to confronting evil, there is always the reality of fear. What fears do you have that your efforts could be thwarted or that you could get in "over your head", or that others might not understand your concern for the issues you identified? How might you counter this fear?

5. Every effort of this nature requires a team. Who do you know in your life who might join you in this venture?

When Evil Overwhelms: A Father and His Boy, (Mark 9: 14 – 29).

Sometimes, encountering evil in the world can be very personal in nature. When churches move into ministries that address some of the most destructive realities at work in people, it is common to come face to face with situations where evil has overwhelmed a person, and where it will seek to overwhelm those who try to confront it. The disciples faced just such a situation, as described in Mark 9, at the very moment that Jesus was up on the mountain of his transfiguration with some of his closest disciples: Peter, James, and John. While they were away, events were afoot that the rest of the disciples were struggling to control. A desperate man had brought his precious son to the disciples seeking help for the episodes of seizures he experienced. But the disciples were not successful in their attempts to heal him. It is clear from the story that what afflicted the boy was more than just what we would today call epilepsy. When Jesus came on the scene, the spiritual entity that tormented the boy threw him into a violent fit that threatened his life. Jesus asked the man how long the boy had been experiencing this. The man answered:

> *"...from childhood. ²² And it has often cast him into fire and into water, to destroy him. But if you can do anything, have compassion on us and help us." ²³ And Jesus said to him, "'If you can'! All things are possible for one who believes." ²⁴ Immediately the father of the child cried out and said, "I believe; help my unbelief!"* (Mark 9: 21b – 24).

This is a moving scene. The father was desperate for help and relief from the unseen forces affecting his family. He had asked the Church — the proto-Church, represented in the disciples — but they were unable to help. The evil was too much for them. And yet, when the situation was finally given to Jesus, he made short work of it, freeing the boy, and returning him to his grateful father. Soon after, the disciples asked Jesus why they were not able to perform this miracle themselves. The answer seems obvious, the Church can never confront evil without Jesus' help and authority. Jesus also told them in verse 29, that this kind of evil can only come out with prayer.

This story gives us some important insights about confronting evil. First, evil will increase when the work of the Kingdom of God becomes more focused. The weeds react when the wheat is on the move. Peter, James, and John had just witnessed the glory of Jesus on the mountain as he was transfigured before them; they even saw Moses and Elijah in the process! We know from Peter's second letter (2 Peter 1: 17 – 18), that this experience stayed with him for the rest of his life, defining his own understanding of Jesus' power and identity. But while the Kingdom was making its appearance, at the foot of the mountain evil was showing its face. First, we discover in verse 14 that the situation had escalated because of an argument between the disciples and the local teachers of the law. When the Church moves to confront evil, especially evil seated in societal problems, there will be differences of opinion resulting from the various ways that people see the issues of the day. One of the key points associated with confronting evil, is knowing how to communicate to others in a way that produces consensus around the values of God's Word, rather than allowing the competing voices of our culture to determine the battlelines of discussion. We do not know what the disciples and the scribes were arguing about, but most likely it was regarding the religious law of Israel and how to proceed with deliverance from an evil presence. Everyone felt they were an expert, and yet no one really knew what to do. This reminds us of how people often approach societal issues today.

Is that not just how we feel when we step into new areas to do ministry, particularly areas that are unfamiliar to us? Suddenly there are all these opinions that need sorting out! Discernment and wisdom are needed to bring people together around the core issues that can be addressed by the promises of God's Kingdom. But most of all, what is needed is Jesus. When Jesus showed up in this story in Mark's Gospel, the conversation became centered, not on everyone's ideas about what was happening, and their competing values and biases, but instead on the specific situation of this father and this boy and how best to help them. In fact, when Jesus showed up, suddenly the actual victims were allowed to speak and define their own situation, apart from how everyone else wanted to define it. Jesus moved forward from there, and it was only because of his intervention that the boy was healed, and the father was relieved of his stress.

This story is such a wonderful picture of what can happen when the Church is truly led by the Spirit of God to cut through all the static, to identify the spiritual problems and to apply the healing that only the Church can give in the authority of Jesus' name.

Notice, the disciples were so moved by Jesus' ability to cut through the confusion and apply the power of the Kingdom of God, that they immediately came to him and asked that important question: *"Why could we not cast it out?" (Mark 9:28).*

This question gets at the heart of so much of the fear associated with the local church confronting evil. We fear failure. We are shy to take on problems that many people before have attempted to address, but with mixed results. In many cases previous efforts have failed, people have come away burned and evil has returned even stronger than before, even more potent in its ability to confuse. When we think of persistent problems in our communities such as generational poverty, substance abuse, crime and violence, and cycles of abuse, we might ask that question of Jesus too: "Why could we not cast it out?" If others have failed over many years, why should we think we could be successful now.

The answer of course is, again, Jesus. This is why his response to his disciples in verse 29 is so important too: *"And he said to them, 'This kind cannot be driven out by anything but prayer'" (Mark 9: 29).* Evil cannot be confronted without prayer, seeking to bring the powerful presence of Jesus. We must turn the situation over to him, as happened in this story when he came down from the mountain. If a church wants to rush in without the hand of Jesus in action, most likely evil will win that battle and return even more reinforced.

But when we quietly and humbly seek Jesus in prayer and bring his authority and discernment into the effort first, we find that Jesus will show the way.

When confronting evil, the Church must always remember that this is ultimately God's battle. This is his field. Jesus explained that clearly in this parable. God has a plan for his field and for the problem of evil. We know that God will win, the Kingdom of God will prevail. How that plays out in and around your congregation depends on the extent to which you and your leaders engage with God's plan to bring relief and release, and ultimately, to bring in the harvest.

CHAPTER 3

The Parable of the Mustard Seed — Investing in Great Potential

"He told them another parable: "The kingdom of heaven is like a mustard seed, which a man took and planted in his field. ³² Though it is the smallest of all seeds, yet when it grows, it is the largest of garden plants and becomes a tree, so that the birds come and perch in its branches."

Matthew 13: 31 – 32

"Hoosiers" is one of the greatest feel-good sports movies of all time. The story it tells is about more than giving people a chance, it is about risking failure to do so. It is betting on the hidden potential in others, because we believe and trust in God's promise that he loves to work with what is small or broken, so that he may reveal his glory. The movie is inspired by the true 'Cinderella story' of a small-town Indiana high school basketball team that won the state championships in 1954.

One important character, an alcoholic named Shooter, played by Dennis Hopper, had failed at most things in his life—but he has an extraordinary knowledge of, and passion for, the game of basketball. The coach, Norman Dale, played by Gene Hackman, works with Shooter to give him a second chance, asking him to be assistant coach.

Under Normal Dale's leadership, the little-known Hickory High School basketball team starts to experience winning ways. During a pivotal game, Gene Hackman's character fakes an argument with the referee in order to get thrown out of the game and force Shooter into the role of replacement coach. In a remarkable scene, Shooter finds a way to shine, and the team wins another game on the way to the state final.

But this is not the only situation in which the coach takes this kind of risk. In another scene, he gives the job of an important free throw to the shortest player on the team, a player who cannot even shoot overhand! Of course, this player makes the basket. The movie takes us all the way to the high school finals in Indianapolis where we witness the climax of the theme of the small overcoming the odds to surprise everyone. If you have not seen it, rent or stream the movie and enjoy the ending in all its feel-good glory!

Similarly, over and over in scripture, we see God's preference for using the small to overcome the big. The childhood of King David is a classic example of this. His faith in God was much bigger than the giant Goliath that he overcame. Another famous story is that of Gideon who defeated the Midianites with the three hundred men, described in Judges 7 and 8. God intentionally whittled down the forces of Israel from many tens of thousands to only three hundred warriors. But there are countless other stories that do not as often make it to the Sunday School 'flannel board'. In the stories of the patriarchs, God worked against cultural norms, often choosing the smallest or youngest of the family to carry on the covenant promise. Here is a powerful passage from Isaiah 41 where God speaks out of parental compassion to "little Jacob":

"But you, Israel, my servant,
Jacob, whom I have chosen,
you descendants of Abraham my friend,
I took you from the ends of the earth,
from its farthest corners I called you.
I said, 'You are my servant';
I have chosen you and have not rejected you.
So do not fear, for I am with you;
do not be dismayed, for I am your God.
I will strengthen you and help you;
I will uphold you with my righteous right hand"
(Isaiah 41: 8 – 10).

And,

"For I am the Lord your God
who takes hold of your right hand
and says to you, Do not fear;
I will help you.
Do not be afraid, you worm Jacob,
little Israel, do not fear,
for I myself will help you," declares the Lord,
your Redeemer, the Holy One of Israel" (Isaiah 41:
13 – 14).

God continues to contrast his greatness and power with the 'littleness' of Jacob, a nickname for the people of Israel. When God uses the word "worm" here it is not a term of disgust or derision; it is a term of endearment. What could a worm do to help itself? It is a pitiful little creature, and yet God lifts up the smallest by applying his great love.

It is from this scriptural foundation that we understand God's preference for the small, the underdog, the oppressed, the poor, the down and out, and the one everyone has counted out of the championships. He wants to reveal himself in the surprise of the small having the greatest impact. His imperative to the church is to follow his lead. Do not discount the small; rather, invest in the small. Believe in the 'upside-down' Kingdom of God, where 'power' is deceptive, and 'weak' means great potential because of God's amazing strength and provision.

This is one of the reasons I have come to love and appreciate small churches. I think God does too. In small churches, the importance of each person's contribution and each person's gifts is amplified by hundreds of times. The first congregation I served was a church of 6,000 members. I was just beginning in ministry when I was on staff there, and I felt like I was part of something really important. On Sundays, a significant portion of the population of the town was affected by the ministry of that congregation. There were seven full-time pastors and a staff approaching thirty people, of which I had the privilege of being one. In fact, I was hired to do youth ministry for just the eighth graders, a group of over one hundred kids! During my time there I felt like I made an impact on the 8th graders, but most likely it was a superficial one. My next church, where I served as an ordained pastor, was smaller; I oversaw the entire youth ministry, roughly one hundred kids. I recognize now that I had considerably more impact on those students than at the church where there were a hundred kids per class. Now, in my current church of under 200 people, with a youth group of around fifteen active kids, I have found my personal discipleship of them is occurring at an even deeper level than in other places.

From a worldly perspective, it might appear that my career is going in the wrong direction. I would disagree. God is trusting me with deeper impact, which happens on the small scale more than on the large scale. Now, I think about all the gifts, ideas and potential Kingdom Impacts that lay dormant in that congregation of 6000. That church was way too large to unlock the Kingdom potential of its people. It is not that only small churches can do this. One of the ways that large churches accomplish deeper impact is by growing *small* to foster a bigger impact. This is how small group ministries work in mid-sized to large churches. Connecting people in smaller and more impactful communities creates a more profound transformation. The idea is to move people from large group experiences like weekend worship, into classes, into small groups, and finally into one-on-one mentoring and faith-sharing. Smaller and smaller contexts imply that much greater things are happening.

When we think about Jesus' ministry, we see again God's preference for the small and concentrated impact. Jesus changed the world by investing in a group of twelve men, and ultimately in a small inner group of three. There were many more people in Jesus' orbit, but those he discipled closely were those inner twelve. His choices of people for that inner group also shone a spotlight on God's inclination for the small and those easily passed over. Jesus chose Galileans for his core ministry team. They were conspicuous for their country accent and unschooled ways. In fact, Jesus started his discipleship group with these fishermen, men who did not immediately command respect in educated circles. I love the description of when the group of disciples arrived together in Jerusalem, as told by Luke in his Gospel. They must have seemed like country bumpkins seeing the big city for the first time: "Look at the big buildings!" (this is a paraphrase of Luke 21: 5). I do the same whenever I visit Chicago. Yet Jesus redirected their focus: *"But Jesus said, ⁶ "As for what you see here, the time will come when not one stone will be left on another; every one of them will be thrown down" (Luke 21" 5b – 6).*

Jesus invested in those whose potential only he could see. Their potential was more in their willingness to trust him, than what they had to offer. Who other than God himself would have started with insignificant fishermen on the Sea of Galilee to begin the most significant chapter of his saving work and plan? Jesus chose the most unlikely characters to form the proto-church. Only Jesus would do that!

The Apostle Paul expressed this principle of the Kingdom in 1 Corinthians 1: 27:

"For the foolishness of God is wiser than human wisdom, and the weakness of God is stronger than human strength. Brothers and sisters, think of what you were when you were called. Not many of you were wise by human standards; not many were influential; not many were of noble birth. But God chose the foolish things of the world to shame the wise; God chose the weak things of the world to shame the strong. God chose the lowly things of this world and the despised things—and the things that are not—to nullify the things that are, [29] so that no one may boast before him. It is because of him that you are in Christ Jesus, who has become for us wisdom from God—that is, our righteousness, holiness and redemption" (1 Corinthians 1: 25 – 30).

When my current congregation formed ten years ago, we sought out mission partners that were small. The idea was, as a small church, we wanted to also partner with small organizations to make an outsized impact. If we could concentrate our giving in this way, making a big splash in small ponds, we might help propel small and young mission organizations to the next level of their ministry. We felt that by doing this we were multiplying the effect that our giving would have. Of course, there is nothing wrong with giving to large, well-established mission organizations. They are doing significant work for the Kingdom of God. But there is something about the small mission project taking on a big challenge that reminded us of how Jesus operates. It reminded us of this parable.

In the Parable of The Mustard Seed, we see that the Kingdom is small and insignificant in the beginning, but Jesus promised it would grow to be a large tree in which many would find shelter.

When he started his ministry, Jesus was only one individual with a radical message, but slowly his message of the Kingdom of God caught the attention of the crowds. But Jesus did not start with crowds. He started in small towns where he preached, taught, and healed. Then he added those twelve unlikely individuals as his core group, training them up in what he was doing. From there, he added the seventy-two, and so on. After his death and resurrection, the Christian movement exploded. But still, it has taken two thousand years to reach where we are today. Jesus even talked about himself using a small metaphor: *"Very truly I tell you, unless a kernel of wheat falls to the ground and dies, it remains only a single seed. But if it dies, it produces many seeds" (John 12: 24).*

And so, it has! Following the resurrection of Jesus and the coming of the Holy Spirit at Pentecost, Christian missionaries moved quickly into the heart of the Roman Empire, led by the Spirit of God. At one point, Paul talked about his intention to go east, but instead, in a vision of a man from Macedonia, he was led west instead, (Acts 16:9). It might be that the early Church's inclination was to avoid Roman power, given that Jesus received a Roman execution. But obedience to God's call took the Gospel directly into the heartlands of the very power structure that crucified Jesus and continued to persecute the early Christians. Though they were small, the early Church effectively conquered the Roman Empire itself. Three hundred years after Jesus' resurrection, the official religion of Rome became Christianity following the conversion of the Emperor Constantine. Today, the Christian faith shelters more people than any other world religion; it shelters a greater variety of people, having touched every land, as Jesus promised it would on the mount of his ascension.

The prophetic message of the Parable of the Mustard Seed is on full display in our day. Jesus asks us to see the way he sees, to see the potential in each person, to see the power of the small and concentrated impact. It is why so many churches help people identify and grow in their spiritual gifts. Those gifts, and that potential, are hidden inside each believer who trusts and follow him.

It was during the Coronavirus quarantine in 2020 that I learned something new about seeds while homeschooling our daughters. I had always wondered how a seed worked. I marveled at how seeds can be coaxed to grow, even those thousands of years old. In one of my daughter's online science lessons, I learned that inside each seed is, in fact, a tiny plant, with a root, stem and tiny leaves, all ready to go. Given the right environment and conditions, that new plant will burst out into the world. Inside each believer, and inside each small organization, is already the bigger impact ready to take shape. This is the miraculous work of the Spirit of God. We must always ask what God might bring forth in a person for greater impact. If this person comes to Christ and discovers the role they can play in God's Kingdom, what might they do to plant, cultivate, and shelter many more? How many does your life shelter right now?

Jesus used birds in this parable, not as the enemy trying to steal the seeds, but as examples of those who will be sheltered as the seed grows into a large plant. These birds are a sign that God wants to reach and shelter so many more. In fact, Jesus may have been drawing on an image from the prophet Ezekiel here:

> *"'This is what the Sovereign Lord says: I myself will take a shoot from the very top of a cedar and plant it; I will break off a tender sprig from its topmost shoots and plant it on a high and lofty mountain. On the mountain heights of Israel I will plant it; it will produce branches and bear fruit and become a splendid cedar. Birds of every kind will nest in it; they will find shelter in the shade of its branches. All the trees of the forest will know that I the Lord bring down the tall tree and make the low tree grow tall. I dry up the green tree and make the dry tree flourish. I the Lord have spoken, and I will do it'" (Ezekiel 17: 22–24).*

What Ezekiel prophesied is the fulfillment of the promise that tiny Israel would become a light to the nations, that Abraham would be the father of many nations as God promised him thousands of years ago, and that his descendants would be as many as the stars in the sky, (Genesis 15:5). But at that point, it was just little Abraham. One man. Yet, inside him was a seed: *"The promises were spoken to Abraham and to his seed" (Genesis 12: 7)*. But as the revelation of God's Word continues, we find, in fact, that the seed of Abraham is Jesus himself. Later, as we come into Jesus through faith and as we are grafted into the family, we become Abraham's seed too: *"If you belong to Christ, then you are Abraham's seed, and heirs according to the promise" (Galatians 3: 29)*. The image here is a succession of seeds, of which Abraham was the first. But planted inside him was the Seed that would establish the Kingdom of God; and now, by faith, we have received that Seed planted inside of us so that we might continue the planting. As I learned just this past year, each seed has that new plant already contained inside its tiny shell. This is all God's work, even witnessed in the natural world.

Following God's vision, we must invest in small and think big. Christian mission believes in, and plans for, outsized impact through faith. That happens when the Spirit of God adds that unseen power to our effort, investment, and prayer. When churches are really moving with God, their impact becomes greater for the Kingdom than their size. We need to start thinking and evaluating our ministries with that goal in mind. If that is not happening, we are just functioning on our own energy and effort. The "God factor" must be in play for the kind of impact Jesus is talking about here. Look again. *"He told them another parable: "The kingdom of heaven is like a mustard seed, which a man took and planted in his field. [32] Though it is the smallest of all seeds, yet when it grows, it is the largest of garden plants and becomes a tree, so that the birds come and perch in its branches" (Matthew 13: 31 – 32)*.

What do you notice that we have not talked about yet? There is a character in this parable that has not been mentioned in our

45

discussion yet. It is the man. The man had to plant the seed. He had to choose the seed and choose the context. Along with faith, both effort and choice are necessary on our part. The man could have looked at the seed and thought: "That is pretty small. It is probably not worth my investment." But farmers know how seeds work, and now, thanks to homeschooling, so do I!

Maybe you look at your congregation today and say: "We are pretty small, what could we really do?" Or you look at your bank account and say: "It's pretty small, what could I really give?" Or, you look at yourself and say: "I only have one gift I can think of, what could I really do?" Jesus gave us this parable to remind us that he is not discouraged by the small. Conversely, he loves it; he even prefers it. He loves surprising a watching world with the outsized impact his people can make.

One of the blessings my congregation had right from the beginning was to be partnered with a small Christian school called Aletheia. They met in the same church building where our congregation originally rented space, serving about thirty families with school-aged children. Part of their vision was to keep class sizes small and to offer Classical Christian education at roughly half the price of the other Christian schools in town. When our church was put in the position to buy the building, it was important to us that Aletheia continued their ministry with us. We believed in what they felt called to do, and we made room for their future growth. We understood that God had enabled our little congregation to purchase a building much larger than we needed, and we felt God's call to not make that building something that we coveted as just our own. We did not want worldly values to guide the mission or vision of our church. Instead, we wanted to continue to make it a place where God was doing *multiple* works. Nor did we did not want the church building's many classrooms to sit empty six days of the week. God has blessed that school and it continues to grow its impact. Families from our congregation have started to enroll their children, further solidifying this important relationship.

What is the mandate that Jesus is giving to the Church in this parable? What is the mustard seed? It is the vision to choose the small and empower it to make a big impact for God's Kingdom. It is seeing the spiritual gift and the spiritual potential lying dormant and waiting for its time. It is the Gospel planted inside one life, that will unleash Kingdom power to transform many and shelter many. It is the God-factor at work in the church to make outsized impact in the world. It is also something that lies dormant and waiting in you, something small that needs only to be chosen.

Here is another way that this parable can be applied right inside the church. When pastors and leadership boards look for ministry leaders we often default to worldly values. We look for people with a proven track record, or the most obvious gifts. To use an Old Testament example, we look for the Saul, when God is preparing the David. When we do this, we stifle greater Kingdom Impact by not choosing how God would choose. Jesus tells us that God loves to use the small. One of the hallmarks of the Kingdom of God is the unlikely person who makes an outsized impact. Is there a person in your life, in your church, or in your place of work, who just needs a chance to shine? It takes faith, but if we default to worldly thinking, we can miss the "Shooter" whom God is now preparing to take over the game.

KINGDOM IMPACT EXAMPLE, INVESTING IN GREAT POTENTIAL: IMAGO DEI CHURCH, PEORIA, IL — THE BREAKFAST CLUB.

Imago Dei Church was founded in Peoria, Illinois, in 2009. It quickly became a unique body of believers, which attracted many young adults. The leaders emphasized strong community engagement and a unique worship style that included a question-and-answer style of teaching. It has grown over the last decade to have a worshipping community of almost three hundred people. Early in its history, the congregation chose to be the kind of church that reached out in tangible ways to portions of the community that are often forgotten, passed over, or intentionally ignored. Today, they have a unique ministry called the Breakfast Club, that serves those experiencing homelessness in the Peoria area. At the time of this writing, they serve breakfast to around one hundred people each Sunday morning right at the church. This started as an effort to bridge the gap in the community. When the Breakfast Club began, there simply were no food shelves or soup kitchens open on Sunday mornings because churches engaged in worship and served their own internal communities on that day. Imago Dei wanted to change that.

Right away we can see how the Breakfast Club fits into the idea of Kingdom Impact, but how is it an example of the small making outsized impact? It has to do with how this ministry started. Back in the first year of Imago's existence, the church rented office space in a building downtown. In that area they encountered a woman who, every week, brought food in the back of her van into Peoria's downtown to feed those without shelter. She was one woman doing everything she could to serve those with whom Jesus identifies: the "least of these", as described in Matthew 25: 40 – 45. Imago's leaders saw this as a chance to partner with a small effort and give it outsized impact. They asked this woman if they could partner with her as a church, providing a place in the church's rented space to serve these breakfasts. This continued as the church grew large enough to purchase its own location.

Today, Imago sends buses out into the community, bringing as many as a hundred folks to the church for breakfast even before the hour of worship on Sundays. Do <u>not</u> miss that. This congregation serves the poor, and those experiencing homelessness, on Sunday mornings even before they gather for worship. Those of us on a church staff know how much time and energy Sunday mornings take on the part of volunteers, alone. Sunday morning is the time to open the building for worship and Bible study, and to make sure it is clean and inviting for all. Normally this is all that churches do on Sunday mornings. But the Breakfast Club changes the focus completely. The breakfast ministry is the first thing. But there is an added consideration: When you bring people into your building that have not had the resources to care well for themselves, or a change of clothes, there are some undesirable realities that can conflict with the goal of making a building clean and appealing for visitors. The part of the building where the breakfast is served has a distinct smell each Sunday morning. It is the smell of the Kingdom of God in action.

Pastor Josh explained this reality: "Imago is a unique group of Christian believers. People don't remain with us at Imago Dei if they don't understand what it is that we are trying to do. We are a church for those who don't easily belong or fit in other churches. Many people come to our church because they have been hurt or rejected in other places. This gives most Imago people a greater sensitivity to those who are on the outside. This is a vision that is really embraced by our whole congregation."

Those who come for the breakfast are invited to stay for worship, but this is not required. The buses return people after breakfast to the places they were picked up from if they choose. But a handful do stay each week and worship with the rest of the congregation. Important relationships have developed here. One gentleman who suffered with mental illness was taken under the wing of a former pastor couple. He came to dinner at their home, celebrated holidays with them and their family, and they helped him find ways to better manage his finances. The COVID-19 quarantine in 2020 did not stop this ministry; instead of bringing people to the building, the church used their buses to take food to those who were living on the street.

The story of Imago Dei's Breakfast Club relates to Jesus' Parable of the Mustard Seed in several ways. First, the congregation partnered with 'the small' to give it much greater impact. This is the power of Kingdom resources put into action and shared freely and generously, rather than kept for the church's own. The fact that this is done on Sunday mornings is one of the best examples of this selfless approach. Not only is it selfless, it is courageous, and courage is a primary component of faith. How many churches would "jeopardize" their potential growth on Sunday mornings by welcoming this population right into their building — not just a few — but a hundred people! No church would follow this plan if it were thinking according to the values of the world and what would market its ministry most effectively. Imago's example reminds us that God's Kingdom does not work according to human values. These are Jesus' values in action.

And that brings us to the next way that this ministry relates to the Parable of the Mustard Seed. Jesus said that once the mustard seed grows into a large plant, many birds will come and find shelter. What a beautiful image of how human beings, made in God's image, might find their place, or as Jesus said, a 'perch' (Matthew 13: 32). This has even greater impact when we realize that Imago Dei is Latin for "the image of God". This must be what the people of Imago Dei see when they serve in the Breakfast club on Sunday mornings.

Discussion Questions:

1. What emotions did the story of Imago Dei's Breakfast Club create in you? Why do you think you reacted in these ways?

2. What do you think it would require for a church to sacrifice Sunday mornings in the way this church has for their breakfast ministry?

3. Are there ministries in your town or area that are small or just getting started, that could use a "leg up", and an excited and encouraging giving partner such as yourself or your congregation?

4. In what ways does your church "shelter" individuals already? How can this be further developed?

5. As you finished reading this chapter, was there a person in your church that came to mind, someone who has been passed over for leadership positions who could be given the chance to grow and shine?

6. What gifts or ideas do you see lying dormant in your church? What ideas have not had the consideration or the investment they need to grow?

7. When have fear or mistrust of the small, held you back from following God's call?

CHAPTER 4

The Parable of the Yeast — Growing Cultural Impact

"He told them still another parable: "The kingdom of heaven is like yeast that a woman took and mixed into about sixty pounds of flour until it worked all through the dough."

Matthew 13: 33

As we work through the different impacts of the Kingdom described by Jesus in Matthew 13, I want to call to attention the phrase he uses to introduce each of the Kingdom parables: "The kingdom of heaven is like…" There is a lot to digest right there. I am suggesting that each of these parables can be used as lenses through which we can evaluate and plan for Kingdom Impact. Of course, these parables are also much more than that, and this parable is a good place for us to acknowledge that bigger view. When Jesus says to us, "The kingdom of heaven is like…" we are reminded that he came to us as the "man from heaven", as is presented in

1 Corinthians 15: 47 – 48. But Jesus also implied it himself, in his late-night conversation with Nicodemus in John, chapter 3. In that discourse, when Jesus was trying to explain spiritual realities to Nicodemus, he said this, *"I have spoken to you of earthly things and you do not believe; how then will you believe if I speak of heavenly things? [13] No one has ever gone into heaven except the one who came from heaven—the Son of Man" (John 3: 12 – 13).*

The irony of this discourse is that, although Nicodemus was a spiritual teacher, he was unable to grasp the concepts that Jesus was communicating to him. This irony was not lost on Jesus, who commented to Nicodemus, *"You are Israel's teacher, and you do not understand these things?" (John 3:10).* We can hear Jesus' observation in various ways. It could be taken as a criticism, as an exhortation, or simply as ironic. It is probably a little of each. But the fact is, Jesus came to earth as the embodiment of the Word of God. In as much as we Christians call the Bible the Word of God, Jesus himself is more so. He is the Living Word, the Word made flesh who came to dwell among us, as it says in John 1:14. Jesus came to reveal to us what heaven really looks like and how heaven really works. And what is heaven? It is God's reality. It is not surprising that Nicodemus did not understand the deep spiritual truths that Jesus was talking about. Nicodemus could not even picture a man being born a second time, let alone the heavenly realities Jesus spoke about. None of us can, until it happens to us, and the perspective of heaven is applied to our lives by God's gracious action.

When Jesus presents these parables, he is speaking as the "man from heaven", the only one who can talk about heavenly realities with the authority of a first-hand witness and bring them into sharp focus for us. But Jesus is not just a witness of heaven's realities, he is, himself, the Creator and Sustainer of them. Therefore, Jesus also has authority to bring those realities to earth. So, here is the conclusion we come to: The Church is the beginning of those heavenly realities manifested on earth. As a member of Jesus' Church, you are called to make those heavenly realities a tangible experience for those you encounter every day. These parables are part of Jesus' vision of how the Church will do just that. But they are also simple statements of fact about the heavenly reality that Jesus will bring fully to earth when he returns. When Jesus says, "The kingdom of heaven is like…" he is speaking both of present realities, as well as God's bright future for humankind. It is the reason that Jesus instructs us to pray in his Lord's Prayer: *"Your kingdom come; your will be done on earth as it is in heaven." (Matthew 6: 10).*

Jesus is the only man who has been to heaven. His mission is to bring heaven's reality here, amongst us, that his Father's will would be done here, just as it is in heaven. If that is true, your church has a powerful mandate: to slowly, but surely, unabashedly and without apology, change the culture of which you are a part to better suit heaven's in-breaking reality. This is the message of The Parable of the Yeast.

In his book *Loving God*, Chuck Colson gave a powerfully-imagined story inspired by the events of a 4th Century AD monk named Telemachus. Telemachus had an enormous cultural impact as the catalyst for changing the nature of what happened in the Colosseum in Rome, and eventually, in all gladiator-type games. His story was first told by the church historian Theodoret, a bishop in Syria. I summarized how Chuck Colson envisioned the story:

> *Telemachus was a simple, honest, and devoted follower of Christ, serving his monastic community by tending their vegetable garden. But then out of the blue he felt Christ's call to go to Rome. He was terrified at the thought. But in prayer Christ pressed him further. Obediently, he packed his belongings and made the trip, unaware of what he was supposed to do there. When he arrived, Rome was celebrating its recent victory over the Goth armies and there was a huge celebration underway. Pious Telemachus never felt so out of place, but he sensed that God's purpose for*

him somehow had to do with the gathered crowds. He allowed himself to be caught up in the throng as it moved through the city. Telemachus had no idea the crowd was headed toward the Colosseum for a gladiator battle. He had never heard of a gladiator before, but as he took his seat and saw the armed men enter the Colosseum floor, he shuddered at the premonition of violence. The gladiators saluted the emperor: "We who are about to die, salute thee". Telemachus began to realize what this show was all about. Men would battle and kill one another for no other reason than to entertainment the crowds. As the battle started, Telemachus felt an enormous courage rise in his heart. He leapt from his seat and ran down to the edge of the arena shouting: "In the name of Christ — stop!" But no one could hear him over the din of the crowd.

Quickly he jumped over the barrier and onto the sand of the arena floor. He yelled louder, "Stop! In the name of Christ, stop! The crowd started to laugh thinking this was part of the show, a funny little monk running between the enormous gladiator men. As he got too close to a duel, one of the fighters knocked Telemachus over with his shield. Telemachus rushed at another duel, trying to get the men to stop. Again, they knocked him over.

But now, the crowd became annoyed at the monk. Someone jumped up on their seat and shouted: "Run him through". Many others in the crowd cheered in agreement. The gladiator obliged, and with one slice, the monk was laid out on the sand in a pool of his own blood. But, not before Telemachus had the chance to yell one more time: "In the name of Christ, stop!"

> *The Colosseum went silent. The tragedy of*
> *Telemachus' death turned the course of public opinion.*
> *No one had expected to see a man of God killed that*
> *day. In the silence, suddenly, people began to leave.*
> *There had been a campaign in recent years, led by*
> *Christians, to pressure Rome's leaders to end the*
> *gladiator battles. But it was the event of Telemachus'*
> *death that changed history. The Christian Emperor*
> *Honorius officially banned gladiator games in honor*
> *of Telemachus, beginning January 1ˢᵗ, 404 AD.*
> *Telemachus was later granted sainthood, the changing*
> *of the culture of the Colosseum being proof of a miracle.*
> *(summarized from Chuck Colson, Loving God)*

In the Parable of the Yeast, Jesus described the special properties of yeast in the way it changes the texture and *expression* of the dough. By consuming sugar and producing carbon dioxide, it transforms the dough from a lifeless lump to a rising batter, filled with delicious smells. Jesus used the miracle of the yeast to show us how God's truth does the same, to work its way through the 'dough': a family, a community, a city, a country, and eventually the world. Slowly, working according to its nature, yeast brings about surprising, lasting, and *pleasing* change. Jesus calls the Church to have growing and lasting cultural impact in the same way.

One of the interesting things about yeast is that it remains hidden until the right time. It is the same color as the rest of the ingredients. Until you add the water and the sugar, you might not notice its presence at all. But soon, the effect of the yeast becomes obvious. The warm delicious smell will bring everyone running. Theologian Michael Green said in his commentary on the Gospel of Matthew: "So it is with the Kingdom. It will pervade society and permeate the whole world." (Green, The Message of Matthew).

Since the Gospel began its spread, wherever it has gone, its effect — the nature and quality of the Kingdom of God — has transformed entire cultures. In its roughly 2000 years, the effect of the Church has been that some of the most brutal and violent peoples on earth have become, instead, among the most peaceful. Societies have been transformed. Now, we cannot say that without acknowledging as well that where the institutional church has become entangled with politics, wealth, and power structures, great evils have occurred. But we are not referring here to the institutional church. Instead, we are talking about the Gospel. Where the Gospel has gone, so has freedom and opportunity, health, education, and order — as well as greater prosperity, compassion, concern for others and morality. The dough rises where the yeast does its work.

One of the metaphors that Jesus applied to himself was "Living Bread". In this study of the Kingdom parables, we see that what Jesus said about himself can also, at times, be said about the Church and its mission. Listen to how Jesus described himself to a hungry crowd in John, chapter 6. This is the same large crowd that he had just fed miraculously with the loaves and fishes. It is now the following day, and they are hungry again. Jesus knows this is the reason they are seeking him: *"...you are looking for me because you ate the loaves and had your fill" (John 6: 26).* Then he went on to explain to them that what they should be looking for was not more food, but more of himself, more Jesus. *"Do not work for food that spoils, but for food that endures to eternal life, which the Son of Man will give you" (John 6: 27).*

Jesus wanted to enact a cultural change in this crowd. Understand what is meant here. Certainly, he wanted to make long-term cultural change in the people of Judea, and ultimately the entire world. But what he confronted in that moment was the culture of that specific crowd. They had been enthusiastic for the things that Jesus was bringing to them. But their hunger for spiritual things was short-lived — about as long as it took for their previous meal to have gone through their digestive systems, requiring another trip to the 'buffet'. Jesus wanted to reorient their hunger toward a more satisfying spiritual meal: himself, the eternal food. He said: *"I am the bread of life. Whoever comes to me will never go hungry" (John 6: 35).*

Every group has a culture; so does every church. When you think of the culture of your church, what comes to mind? What is valued in the culture of your congregation? What is expected of leaders? What does it take to get into leadership? What does the culture of your church see as most often at stake? Is it money, influence, power, the facility, a certain tradition, or a way of worshipping? Families have a culture; so does a workplace and a circle of friends. These micro-cultures all need to be leavened by the person of Jesus. Jesus wants to impact these cultures with the culture of the Kingdom of God. As we said before, what is true of Jesus, is often true of his Church. You are the source of the leaven to lift the culture of your family, your workplace, your school, and yes, your congregation. The leaven is the Gospel, and it is the truth of God that you are called to sprinkle into the mix. The hard part is getting it started, but once that warm, wonderful odor starts to spread, it will become unstoppable.

In the seminary I attended, one of the things we were taught is that spiritual leaders are 'atmosphere' architects. We have this responsibility to make sure that the character of God is expressed in the nature and atmosphere of the groups of which we are a part. The atmosphere of the room in which we meet should honor God; it should reflect the values of the Kingdom. Spiritual leaders are taught to be sensitive to the feeling of a room and then to transform it with the presence of Christ himself. When you consider the various cultures of which you are a part, is the grace, love, and compassion of God carrying the day? Or is there spiritual *static* in the air, tension, division, or even anger? Are people feeling isolated, agitated, or hurt? The yeast of the Kingdom needs to address all that.

That is one of the reasons that I am so careful about how members of a church treat one another. We must be vigilant where the atmosphere is infected by criticism, judging, or just plain meanness. We cannot allow that in Jesus' Church. I have talked with our leaders about how destructive it is when people "start fires in the corner of the church" through gossip or destructive complaining.

It is important that the concerns and worries of church members are addressed and heard; church leaders need to be transparent and humble, not protective of position. But it is up to everyone in a congregation to foster a healthy, supportive, and truthful culture, and to not participate in those corner conversations. Satan loves the corner. It is where he does his best work.

You carry the yeast. You are the yeast in your neighborhood. Think about your street. How is it different because of the witness for Christ you bring there? What do your neighbors see of Christ in your comments and encouragements, your posts on social media, your concern, your humorous stories, your statements of values? What happens when you invite your neighbors into your home to enjoy food around your table or to just chat? The yeast does its work there. Remember, the yeast effects the flavor, the feel, and the aroma. Fresh and living bread is almost irresistible.

Here is the Apostle Paul expressing the effect of the yeast Jesus refers to: *"For we are to God the pleasing aroma of Christ among those who are being saved and those who are perishing. To the one we are an aroma that brings death; to the other, an aroma that brings life. And who is equal to such a task? Unlike so many, we do not peddle the word of God for profit. On the contrary, in Christ we speak before God with sincerity, as those sent from God"* (2 Corinthians 2: 15 – 17).

As Christians, we are called to be part of the slow but rising cultural influence of the Kingdom of God. This can happen in micro-cultures: families, friendship groups, and your church, as well as macro-cultures: your neighborhood and beyond. Individually, we can have much more immediate cultural influence in smaller places, but the effect of a congregation, a community of people acting intentionally and resiliently can, over time, make a significant and lasting change in a neighborhood and even a city. Over time, concerted effort driven by easily demonstrated values, can introduce a new culture that those outside the church will recognize as positive and mutually beneficial. This is great 'P.R.' for the Kingdom of God, and it is the power of the image Jesus used in this parable.

Yeast is itself a 'culture'. What determines culture on a macro-scale, is just the pressure and impact of a consensus of cultures at the micro-level. Often, as in the case of yeast, it simply depends upon what is growing consistently over time. When yeast is introduced to a batter where the appropriate nutrients are available, the culture will immediately and relentlessly do its thing.

This happened in a small way when my current congregation started to work intentionally in the neighborhood where we set up Jacob's Well and started to offer after-school tutoring and community-based youth ministry. Prior to this there had been very few places that teenagers could gather. Often, they just ended up playing in the streets or moving through properties that were not their own. Some had been causing trouble, getting into fights, or just causing mischief. In more extreme cases, some of these students were becoming involved in the drug culture that existed in the neighborhood as well. That was the culture that was growing at the time.

When these students became involved in Jacob's Well, and were impacted by Christian adults who were intentionally mentoring them through ministry efforts, things began to change. We learned through members of the community (and through the rental office) that there had been a noticeable drop in the kind of behaviors described above. Everyone knew that kids were getting into trouble because they had little to do to occupy their young minds. But when the church got involved, and Biblical values, and more Christ-like examples were put into the mix, the culture started to change.

When we initially began our investigation into the neighborhood, we started talking with local parents about the needs in their community. We discovered that many of the families were believers. One man said prophetically, "There are a lot of believers in this community, if we all got together, there is no telling what could happen!" His sons were among the first to join the new culture happening at Jacob's Well. They became central to the effort, bringing their friends and promoting events the church was doing. That was a critical piece of the puzzle, and a great example of how mission efforts tend to work worldwide. Local leaders are the key to success. Our church could never have accomplished the changes that were taking place without the yeast grains that were already in the mix prior to our arrival. In fact, one could argue that the people from our congregation who started the ministry were not, in fact, the yeast. Instead, we may have been the food that fed the yeast which God had already put into the dough. That man and his boys were among that yeast. Our church's community ministry just fueled what had always been part of God's call for their lives to help change their community. This is a humbling thought. The temptation is always to want to say, "Hey, look at what we did!" But the Gospel moves us in a different direction. The true message is always: "Hey, look what God did!" We were just the *consumable* in the reaction the Spirit of God had prepared earlier.

This is the attitude that Christians should have when we enter any kind of mission, whether it is local, national, or international. We are always working cross-culturally in outreach. It requires lots of time and research to understand the local language and the local ways. And ultimately, we must be humble enough to work with the local change-agents that God put in place long before we showed up. This important mission principle is hidden in a passage from Ephesians where Paul explains that Christian ministry and mission is never our work anyways: *"For it is by grace you have been saved, through faith—and this is not from yourselves, it is the gift of God— [9] not by works, so that no one can boast"* (Ephesians 2: 8 – 9).

God is not looking for ministers who want to boast. If we are not willing to be simply a consumable in the building of his Kingdom, then he will pass us by and search for those who are willing. In his earthly ministry, Jesus saw himself as a consumable in the plan of God: *"Very truly I tell you, unless a kernel of wheat falls to the ground and dies, it remains only a single seed. But if it dies, it produces many seeds" (John 12: 24).* Jesus was willing to make himself nothing (Philippians 2: 7), to accomplish the salvation and the renewal of the human race. The same mindset is required of us if we want to become cultural change agents.

An Important Juxtaposition

Jesus presented The Parable of the Yeast in partnership with his Parable of the Mustard seed. If you read it again, you will see that one sentence basically flows into the next. Yeast grains and mustard seeds have lots in common. Both are small and, in the end, both result in something greater: a large garden plant that birds can perch in, and a warm and delicious loaf that many may enjoy. Both parables contain this message: It is in the small that the greatest work is done. Do you want to win your neighbors to Christ and have them come to church? Be kind and considerate to them. Change the culture. Express concern for their worries and needs. Stand with them, spend time with them. God will do the rest. You are a grain of yeast with great potential to change a culture. You are God's cultural change-agent. You also need to be a willing consumable, willing to die daily, giving sacrificially of your time, energy, and other resources, so that others will live.

Let us get more personal and talk about the culture of our families. What is the atmosphere and the spirit of your household? Does it have that wonderful yeasty smell, the kind that brings people running to the bakery? Do people just love being in your home, including those who live there? Is your home a gentle and safe place, characteristic of the nature of Christ? Or is it a place where family members feel attacked or insecure? The yeast must do its work even in our own homes. If you are a parent, it is your spiritual responsibility to take stock of the yeastiness of your home. You have headship of that home; you are the pastor of your family. Arrange the atmosphere to promote the Kingdom's values. Let Kingdom Impact happen within the walls of your house. Trust God's Word to do its work to change your family's culture.

Here are two wonderful passages from Colossians that I often use with couples getting married when we talk about the nature of a Christian home.

> *"Therefore, as God's chosen people, holy and dearly loved, clothe yourselves with compassion, kindness, humility, gentleness and patience. Bear with each other and forgive one another if any of you has a grievance against someone. Forgive as the Lord forgave you. And over all these virtues put on love, which binds them all together in perfect unity. Let the peace of Christ rule in your hearts, since as members of one body you were called to peace" (Colossians 3: 12 – 15).*

> *"Love must be sincere. Hate what is evil; cling to what is good. Be devoted to one another in love. Honor one another above yourselves. Never be lacking in zeal, but keep your spiritual fervor, serving the Lord. Be joyful in hope, patient in affliction, faithful in prayer. Share with the Lord's people who are in need. Practice hospitality. Bless those who persecute you; bless and do not curse. Rejoice with those who rejoice; mourn with those who mourn. Live in harmony with one another. Do not be proud, but be willing to associate with people of low position. Do not be conceited" (Romans 12: 9 – 16).*

These are two passages that an atmosphere architect should pay attention to! They show you how to design your family to let the yeast work. Yeast needs the right environment to perform its work, or it will remain dormant. That is the case with the characteristics of the Kingdom of God as well. It does not matter what you say you believe, if the way you behave does not let the yeast do its thing. All that potential for warm, pillowy goodness is lost in the dough and the bread will be flat once it is baked.

Are you concerned about the culture of your congregation? You may be key to the change that God wants to bring. Just like a neighborhood that needs its residents to be spiritual leaders, your family can be the yeast that brings a change to your church. As we discussed before, many churches struggle with a tense or even toxic culture of criticism, back-biting, gossip, or mistrust of leadership. Often that culture has been present for a long time. But honest and open discussion of positive change, incrementally, can create a larger dialogue that everyone wants to get in on. Your church leaders are, of course, key to that change. Working around them can make the situation worse. Working with them, honoring their position, can inspire them to do the same for you, to honor the position God is giving you as a change-agent.

Most likely, many people in your church want to see a culture change. But fear often holds the constructive conversations back. Especially, there can be the fear of upsetting others, or stepping on toes, or making the general situation worse and getting blamed in the process. But yeast does not think like that. A yeasty perspective is one that understands itself to be a consumable. Satan's destructive intentions are undone in any congregation in conflict when everyone is willing to die to themselves in the process. He has no remedy for that!

It is healthy families that change churches; it is healthy churches that change neighborhoods, and eventually entire cities. Our country right now is struggling in its culture. Unity in the United States is under enormous attack. Few of us would say that the national dialogue in America is anything but toxic. Divisions are running right through families and right through the hearts of churches as well. What it will take is the courage of individual people to bring what the love of Jesus always brings, a cultural change, the surprising new language of love and grace. We are all yeast grains right now, waiting for the food that will feed a new and more positive culture. Satan's intention to divide Americans, and divide churches, will only be thwarted when we recognize that the real enemy is not fellow citizens. It may be that only the Church in America can bring the cultural change that works across divisions.

Here is an example: In 2018, the power of the yeast was on display in America. Christians networked together across the country to have cultural impact. People who support both major political parties took to social media or made phone calls, calling the White House to end the separation of children from their parents when detained at the border. The effort was so extensive that getting through on the line was almost impossible. And yet, miraculously, the president changed his course and his tone. The national dialogue changed around this issue. This is an example of the power of yeast, the power of truth when spoken to power. Things become much clearer when the moral majority speaks morally. The yeast made its impact. The question is, will this be a long-term cultural change, or just a momentary one? One news source responded to the issue of child separation with something akin to this: "We need to remind people that these are not *our* children being separated from their parents. Like it or not, these are not *our* kids. Show them compassion, but it's not like these are kids from Idaho or Texas… These are children from another country!"

Implication? They matter less. The yeast has a lot more work to do yet.

Kingdom Impact Example, Growing Cultural Impact: New Beginnings Church, Peoria, IL —Bridging the Gap Between Minority Communities and Law Enforcement.

New Beginnings Church began in 2013 under the leadership of Pastor Martin Johnson, with the goal of becoming, a traditional Pentecostal-style church. They started meeting in an industrial park, offering Sunday morning and midweek worship. Looking back, Pastor Johnson indicated that their initial goal was to find a "nice" place where people could worship God. Over a period of three years the church grew from seven members to fifty under this format. The congregation had a heart to do outreach ministry, but given their location, they had to travel to the inner city to minister to people who lacked basic necessities. They created an annual outreach event to downtown Peoria, returning to the safety of the church building with the intention of returning the following year.

This garden-variety approach to mission was upended when it came time for New Beginnings to find a new place to meet. Again, their numbers had grown, and they were financially ready to make the move. But where to locate? They looked at literally every empty building around the Peoria area. Then, after taking a wrong turn one day, Pastor Johnson came across a potential location: an old Rent-A-Center building for sale in the East Bluff neighborhood. He was immediately skeptical. This was an area known for criminal activity. There were five bars within view of the location, and while he sat in the parking lot pondering, he witnessed a drug deal right in front of him. Pastor Johnson's initial sense was that this was not a good location for their church.

But while he was driving away, he felt the Spirit of God direct him back to the property. He decided to share the location with his wife, believing she would confirm his thoughts and easily dismiss it as the future location for the church. But instead, she encouraged him to listen to God. She too felt it was time to locate where the church could have an impact in the community outside of its front doors.

When Pastor Johnson invited key leaders to tour the potential new location, they had a difficult time seeing the vision. Instead, all they could see were spider webs and mildew. When he asked for their reactions to the building, the members tried to be polite and not hurt his feelings, but it was obvious they were not on board with this location. Pastor Johnson went home dejected and upset, but after more prayer and reflection he moved in obedience to God's promptings. He called another meeting with the entire congregation and was open with them about his own misgivings, yet he felt that God was calling them to this place. He expressed his deep conviction that the relocation of New Beginnings was to be a matter of obedience to God, not of fear, or even conventional decision-making. He thanked the members for all that they had done for the church up to that point in time. He shared that if anyone did not feel that God was calling them to make this move, he would write them a letter of recommendation to join another fellowship. Then, he took a vote and said, "Those who believe God is calling you to connect with this new vision, please stand." To his tearful surprise, every member stood in agreement with the decision to move the church to the East Bluff neighborhood.

This step of obedience led New Beginnings Church to a dramatic new level of Kingdom Impact. In Pastor Johnson's words, they moved from a "congregational mindset" to a "Kingdom mindset". The church immediately embraced their new mission by establishing an annual community outreach event called, "Community Fest". This was an event hosted by the church to build relationships, meet needs in the church's community, and communicate the Gospel. This annual outreach event drew hundreds of people to the church property. As they got to know the needs of the community better, the church birthed a food pantry and clothing ministry.

In another simple effort to make a difference, members of the church started to walk the neighborhood every summer Saturday to pick up trash and engage the neighbors. The called this effort "Operation Make-A-Difference". Pastor Johnson explained that the church's message and objective were simple: "We care! We want to show the neighborhood that the church is a part of the community and willing to work together." In these efforts, they began to form genuine relationships and communicated their vision for community transformation through door-to-door conversations. In addition, the neighbors began to participate and take pride in their neighborhood as well.

While the reputation of New Beginnings continued to grow as a church that really cared about the neighborhood and was coming to know members of the community well, God began to propel the church into a very specific role in relationship with law enforcement. Criminal activity was one of the constant issues in the area. Particularly since in the mid-2000s, homicides had been on the increase due to gang and drug activity. Hostilities between the African American community and law enforcement were becoming volatile.

A critical event happened right in front of New Beginnings Church that became a catalyst to repair the fractured relationship between the African American community and the police department. That event was a tragic car accident. An Hispanic woman and her young son had been the victims of a hit and run accident right in front of the church building. The woman had suffered a serious injury. Her foot had been severed and was only hanging by soft tissue. Pastor Johnson rushed to the scene. Using his military training, and with the help of a passer-by, he fashioned a tourniquet with his belt to stop the bleeding and prevent her from going into shock. The paramedics arrived and began to administer aid. When the police arrived, they immediately began to disperse the crowd and set up crime scene tape around the area.

The officer in charge asked the crowd that had gathered if anyone had seen the accident. When the people answered "no", the police officer became frustrated and spoke in a disrespectful manner, angering the crowd. Pastor Johnson stepped in to help. He identified himself as the pastor of the church in front of which they were standing. But when he also indicated he had not witnessed the accident, the officer told him that he also needed to leave. This escalated the situation further. Pastor Johnson had served as an auxiliary sheriff deputy and he understood that the officer was just trying to control the scene. Yet, Pastor Johnson wanted to use this opportunity to bring the police department to a greater level of accountability so that they would also be respected by community members. He calmed the crowd and informed the officer that he would be filing an official complaint with the Police Department because of the way the situation was handled.

Within an hour, command officers arrived to apologize for the incident. The following day, Pastor Johnson received calls from a City Council Representative and the Mayor asking him to meet with the Chief of Police to discuss what had happened. After explaining how he had been treated, especially how the actions of the officer had only added to the sense of disenfranchisement that the community already felt, the police department again responded with an apology. This opened the door for Pastor Martin to become, in his words, "a repairer of the breach".

Pastor Johnson shared that one of the objectives of their church outreach events had been to build relationships. He told the Chief that it would help if his officers came to the events, not as police personnel, but instead as part of the community. Pastor Johnson assured him that the church felt safe in the community and did not need the officers to provide security. Instead, when officers showed up to the events, a member of the church would introduce them as a friend rather than an enemy.

This began to change the culture of the relationship between law enforcement and the community members. From that point on, police officers began to know people by name, young and old alike. When officers came across young people participating in borderline activity, they were able to encourage them to choose right, because they had a previous relationship. The "us vs them" mentality was changing to a "we" mentality.

Pastor Johnson quickly became recognized as a key player in efforts to improve the relationships between minority communities and law enforcement. Now when critical and controversial issues take place in the community, Pastor Johnson is contacted for the purpose of accountability and to help communicate and provide clarity to the community at large. He is trusted on both sides of the law enforcement divide as an ambassador who will help ensure a just result. He has become a bridge builder and a community pastor.

Pastor Martin Johnson is continuing this journey with the Peoria Police Department to help bring long-term change to the way minority communities are understood by officers, and conversely, how officers are understood and received by minority communities. Particularly, he is involved in retraining for officers who need help to reorient their approach to police work, helping them win friends among the African American community. Currently there is an intentional move in the Peoria police to transition from a 'lock them up' approach, to a community policing effort that is more proactive and relational. In Pastor Martin's words: "In this journey we will not exploit one another's weaknesses. We want to see one another's humanity and let that be the way forward."

The story of New Beginnings is one of a church really living up to its name. While the congregation sought a new beginning when they needed to purchase a building, God had something bigger in mind: a new beginning where a local congregation could become a catalyst toward greater understanding in an area of high tension, and a leader in one of the hot-button issues of our day.

The story of these new beginnings is ongoing and accelerating. Other churches are taking notice. Pastor Martin is often in conversation with church leaders who are seeking greater understanding of this model of cultural transformation. While many hundreds of people continue to come to their Community Fests, these events are co-sponsored by other churches as well. Remarkably, New Beginnings Church, a congregation of 125 members, recently purchased an old school in the area and turned it into a community center. They are holding weekly events for kids, as well as educational and sporting events, and ministries to high-risk young adults. Moreover, they continue to serve over 100 families a week at their food pantry. Not only have they helped to make a cultural shift, but they are also making an impact far greater than the size their membership would suggest.

Pastor Johnson has truly become a community pastor. People who are not officially part of New Beginnings Church see him as their pastor and refer to him as so. Elected officials come for discussion about the nature of these issues in Peoria; other pastors come to him for confidential discussions about the future of their ministries. Pastor Martin summed it up: "All this happened because a church that wanted to be comfortable and exist within its four walls, decided instead to submit to the will of God. The church will never go back to being isolated in its own desires and needs."

Discussion Questions:

1. What struck you most about the story of New Beginnings?

2. The issues between minority communities and law enforcement are a flashpoint all over our country. Where did you feel most challenged in your own views while reading this story?

3. Make a list of the cultural changes that the Kingdom of God could make in your city. What attitudes and biases need changing so that people can come together for positive change? Could you see your congregation leading the way in this? How?

4. We have talked about how cultural change can happen at many levels. While it is overwhelming to think about taking on some of the most obvious issues of our day, how might you, as a follower of Jesus, impact the culture of your neighborhood?

5. When you look at just your own street, what cultures do you see at work there? Here are some possible observations: disengaged affluence, conflict in relationships, racial tensions, poverty, racial disengagement, family strife, spiritual poverty, isolation… How might the culture of God's people address these areas of brokenness and bring a stronger, more unified, and positive atmosphere?

6. How would you put into the words the call of the Church to make cultural impact?

7. Are their churches in your community that you see making this level of impact?

CHAPTER 5

The Parables of the Pearl and the Treasure — Uncovering Hidden Value

"The kingdom of heaven is like treasure hidden in a field. When a man found it, he hid it again, and then in his joy went and sold all he had and bought that field. ⁴⁵ "Again, the kingdom of heaven is like a merchant looking for fine pearls. ⁴⁶ When he found one of great value, he went away and sold everything he had and bought it."

Matthew 13: 44 – 46

There was an old buckeye tree outside the back door of my home church in Waterloo, Ontario. In that region it is called a "horse chestnut". If you are familiar with buckeye trees, they produce large, spiny fruits, which contain a nut about the size of a ping pong ball. Each fall when our youth ministry started up, we collected these nuts for a game we called "chestnut wars". It is not what you are imagining. If you hurled this heavy, spiny fruit at a human target it could do some real damage. Instead, we cracked open the fruit to reveal the nut. Each kid had his own secret process for fashioning his weapon. Some would freeze the nuts to harden them; some would bake them to dry them out; some would just let them weather over time. When they were good and hard, our dads would drill a hole in them just large enough for a knotted shoelace to pass through. Then, with our pockets filled with these nuts on shoelaces, we went to school anticipating conquest at recess time. When the bell rang, we gathered at a shallow pit in the school yard to face off against one another. One boy would lay his chestnut in the pit, while the other would whip his down upon it, trying to crack his opponent's chestnut in half. If you beat your opponent, you faced another winner until finally, a fall champion was crowned.

One autumn Sunday, I was walking to church when this golden glint caught my eye. Investigating, I discovered a partially buried chestnut, or what remained of one from a previous year, most likely buried by a squirrel. The shiny, dark brown skin had been scraped off, revealing this pale, shrunken, and shriveled chestnut. It looked like a giant, golden raisin. I plucked it from the ground and discovered it was hard as a rock. I knew I had a treasure, my pearl of great price.

My dad broke two drill bits getting the hole through this ancient chestnut, but by Monday I had my champion in my pocket, ready to take on any challenger. No one could beat me. Of course, I could not do any damage at all to the nuts of the other boys; there was just no weight to this thing at all. But each time they were on the offensive, their chestnuts just split in half, cracking open on my ancient, weather-beaten, chestnut. I was crowned chestnut king that year. It is amazing what such a small triumph can do for the self-esteem of a junior high boy.

Jesus' Parables of the Hidden Treasure and the Pearl of Great Price are both about the experience of finding something of life-changing value. The man who finds the treasure in the field goes and sells everything he owns to purchase that field and possess the treasure. Likewise, the merchant sells all he has to own the pearl.

The key to this parable is the valuing of this treasure as greater than the sum-total of everything a person already has.

Everyone has dreamed of striking it rich. We imagine multiple problems in our lives evaporating simply with more financial resources at our disposal. While evidence tends to show that more money just introduces its own set of problems and stresses, we hold onto this romantic notion that a surprise windfall could make us happy, or happier. The people of Jesus' day must have had the same thought, or he would not have introduced one of his Kingdom parables in this manner. The Parables of the Pearl of Great Price and the Hidden Treasure are really the same parable, stated twice.

The key element in these parables has to do with how human beings define value. Maybe you have heard the classic youth group question, designed to expose what we value: "If you could only take one thing with you to a deserted island, what would you bring?" Then, of course, you feel guilty if a Bible was not the first thing that comes to mind. Normally, I just say I would bring my phone, as it would have the Bible as well as hundreds of sources of entertainment. (Wise youth leaders rule out cell phones as an acceptable answer in that scenario).

If we are honest, perceived worth or value is what drives most of our decisions in life. What is worth my time? What is worth my available cash? Who is worth calling a friend, and what is worth sacrificing for a friend in need? Is this job opportunity worth the education or training I have received? Is this house worth the price? If the values do not add up, that will drive our decision. It is only faith that might mess with that equation when God calls us to do something based, not on earthly values, but on heavenly values. As in the case of New Beginnings Church, if they were looking simply at investment value versus returns, the property in the East Bluff neighborhood was probably not the right place to buy. But as we saw, God's plans and values proved to be much better.

That is why these two parables are so unique. While the other parables in Matthew 13 represented situations that have stood in contrast to worldly values, these two parables appeal to some of the basic wiring of human beings. If I found that treasure or that pearl, I would go after it too. But would I invest all I had? That is the provocative question that these two parables present. Would I risk it all?

Like the MasterCard commercials from a few years back, the treasure Jesus describes here is far more than just a windfall – it is "priceless". So, what is he referring to? Well, there are two different, and equally compelling, interpretations of this parable about the Kingdom of God. One is the idea that the Kingdom of God is something that is so good, and has such value, that it is worth giving up everything to have it. When a person realizes all that God offers: forgiveness of sins in the past, present, and future, eternal life, adoption into his people, and participation in his mission; that person will leave behind every other pursuit, and count as worthless everything else they have, to acquire the Kingdom and to be part of it.

The Gospel is priceless. Jesus did what no one else had the right or ability to do. Jesus purchased for us our salvation, our forgiveness, our right-standing before the Father. Jesus himself said in Matthew 16: *"For whoever wants to save their life will lose it, but whoever loses their life for me will find it. What good will it be for someone to gain the whole world, yet forfeit their soul? Or what can anyone give in exchange for their soul?" (Matthew 16: 25 – 26).*

Jesus places enormous value on even one person's soul. What could a person give in exchange for it? The human soul is the intangible person, the personality, the 'being' we encounter in each person. The soul contains every person's memories as well as the things they hope and dream for. Each soul is uniquely created by God to be part of his good and perfect will. Christian theology puts a high value on people as the "crown" of God's creation.

Think of the contrast between how God values people and the value we place on human life today. We are learning a lot in our culture about human trafficking, its rising statistics globally, and how communities in the United States are among the places to which trafficked people are smuggled. Tragically, in the case of human trafficking, a monetary value is assigned to human beings, so they may be bought and sold 'as is'. But people are dehumanized today in many ways. You do not have to search the dark underbelly of society or the internet to find evidence of it, either. We devalue others when we label them as immigrant, minority, Republican or Democrat, liberal or conservative, or whatever label you might use to put someone into a convenient box. Think of how cheaply we value others for simply having an opposing view in some hot-button topic. We willingly define them and discount them.

In contrast, Jesus put such high value on human beings that he became one of us. He stepped into our human experience so he may enter our suffering and give his life for us. He counted his life as nothing; he gave his all, everything he had, to possess us. He did all this so that, as we place our faith in him, he can share his inheritance with us as the Son of God. No one offers what Jesus offers. No one — period.

And that is what leads us to the second compelling interpretation of the parable. The merchant in the story who sold everything to possess the pearl, the man who discovered the treasure and was willing to trade all his money and possessions to purchase the field — that man is Jesus. The pearl of great price is you. Jesus paid it all so he may have you as his treasure. Now that is some good news!

Really these two interpretations are two sides of the same coin. Maybe that is why Jesus told the same parable twice using different images. Jesus values people as treasure, and once we receive him, we value him so much that we would give all we have, and count everything as a loss, compared to him.

The Apostle Paul expressed this same conviction in his letter to the Philippians. Paul had just given his resumé regarding all the value he once placed in his own credentials as a righteous man according to Jewish law, things he once believed made him better, or more *right* than others. But when he met Jesus, his perspective was turned on its head regarding what God really values: *"But whatever were gains to me I now consider loss for the sake of Christ. [8]What is more, I consider everything a loss because of the surpassing worth of knowing Christ Jesus my Lord, for whose sake I have lost all things. I consider them garbage, that I may gain Christ [9]and be found in him, not having a righteousness of my own that comes from the law, but that which is through faith in Christ—the righteousness that comes from God on the basis of faith"* (Philippians 3: 7 – 9).

Paul considered all his personal assets to be nothing compared to the value of knowing Christ and all that he received spiritually in relationship with him. How can you put a price tag on peace with God, peace with others, and peace with yourself? Is that not what every self-help and self-improvement program is seeking, and selling? And, of course, you must pay for those. But what Jesus gives us is at the same time, both priceless and free. The Gospel is priceless, but thanks to Jesus, it is free to you and me by faith.

Returning to the other side of the coin, it is because Jesus values you and me in this way that our necessary response is to assign every other person the same value, regardless of background, belief, or behavior. Jesus valued them and died for them just as he did for you and for me.

One of the directives this parable gives to the Church is to come around to Jesus' way of seeing people: to give our everything to see the value in other human beings Jesus' way. He calls us to join him in valuing people so much that we would spend ourselves on them, underscoring their worth to Jesus and the Kingdom of God. What does your church spend, give up, and count as nothing, so that you might demonstrate their worth and win people to Christ? This is the test associated with these two parables. What would you give so that you could gain one soul for God's Kingdom? Does your church pass that test?

But there is the deeper question, the question behind the question. A church that does this well — discovering the hidden worth in people — will transfer that worth to them in a way they can *experience* personally. When a new person comes to your church, do they feel and experience their worth in the Kingdom and discover their value to God? Here are a few titles that the New Testament gives to a person who comes to faith in Jesus Christ: beloved of God, temple of the Holy Spirit, servant of the Most High, holy, blameless, a citizen of heaven, a new creation. What is all that worth? It is priceless.

So far, we have looked at the stories of a few churches, just in one small geographical area, that are already motivated in their decision-making by seeing other people as treasures in God's eyes. The churches we have referenced have counted as priceless: the orphan or fatherless child, the refugee or asylum-seeker, the person without shelter, and the minority individual facing prejudgment from law enforcement. The powerful message of this set of two parables of the treasure and the pearl, is that Jesus now throws us all into the mix. We are all greatly valued. Jesus treasured us and gave his all to have us as his own.

Motivated by this God-assigned value, we can make Kingdom Impact by investing intentionally to unlock the hidden worth and value in people. Especially, your congregation can reach into the lives of people in the community that are normally passed over because they have been labeled in a negative way or fall into a category that is easily dismissed. In the previous chapter associated with the mustard seed, we talked about giving people who are already inside our churches a chance to use their gifts, offering leadership opportunities to those who have not yet been chosen. In this chapter, we hear the challenge to seek value in the life of the person outside the church. We are invited to treasure what is found there, to uncover it, and present that value to the person as a gift from the Kingdom of God.

In the last few years, my congregation has developed a fledgling ministry, a career mentoring program called Tekton. Tekton is the Greek word for "builder", and it is the term used in the New Testament to describe Joseph's career, Jesus' stepfather. We can assume this was the career that Jesus was mentored in prior to his earthly ministry. We established Tekton to address a challenging transition time in the lives of young people when they often drift from the ministry of the church — the senior year of high school into the years of their early twenties. There is much to distract young adults at that age: new relationships, new responsibilities, the pressure of graduating, entering adulthood, and choosing university or other career training. At the same time, the youth ministry of their home church may no longer seem as relevant to them as it did when they were a freshman or sophomore. They are transitioning into young adulthood and the church needs to transition with them.

Tekton targets young adults during that transition who are having trouble making decisions about their career path, or who are struggling to navigate important milestones in their continued development. The first couple of years in the program, a few of the early twenty-somethings we worked with had yet to get a driver's license or complete their GED. These students were matched with adult mentors from the congregation who had careers that mirrored some of the students' stated interests. We developed a series of ten, two-hour seminars, to supplement the work the participants were engaged in with their mentors around their life and career goals.

The idea for Tekton originated with a recently retired man in our congregation who had been successful in his career working with manufacturing plants. During his career, Doug interviewed many applicants whom he could have hired if they had just a little more direction and coaching earlier in life. They were missing habits of consistency and follow-through, soft skills related to communication, and how they presented themselves in a professional environment. These were assets that other applicants naturally picked up from better role-modeling at home and in other places. But in his retirement, Doug felt God calling him to invest in the kind of applicant that he had always regretted having to pass over in favor of more prepared individuals. He wanted to get out in front of the problem of young people with deficits in these areas. Tekton was born of this call. This ministry is still in its infancy, but the goal is to recognize the treasure and call out the value that is hidden and buried in so many emerging adults.

The mandate that comes from these two parables is a harder one to fulfill or even conceptualize. It is typically not something that is done on a large scale because it is an intensive ministry over the long-term that brings out the hidden treasure and value in individual people, allowing them to see themselves through God's eyes. Most churches are not going to have a ministry called: "Our ministry to uncover the hidden treasure in people". More than likely, this process occurs in many parts of a congregation's outreach *and* in-reach, more often in an informal setting, where mentoring is happening on a whole lot of fronts and at many different levels. It is a unique church that would understand instinctively how to live out this parable. It is releasing the beauty that God placed in every life when he created people in his own image.

Jesus' Personal Example of Uncovering Hidden Value

Undoubtedly, Jesus is the best person, and the best example, of what it looks like to bring out the value in people. In the Gospels there are many wonderful examples of Jesus going out of his way, even to places where those closest to him did not want him to go, to reach just one person and to put their value on full display. I want to give us three amazing examples from Jesus' ministry:

The Story of Zacchaeus, (Luke 19: 1 – 10)

You are singing the song already, so let us get this over with: *"Zacchaeus was a wee little man"*. But he was not so small as to miss garnering attention. In his hometown of Jericho, he was known for the abuses of his position as a tax collector. If we are inclined to give Zacchaeus the benefit of the doubt that it was just the sordid reputations of his peers in the industry that painted him in this light,

Zacchaeus' own words in verse 8, expose the truth of his crimes. But how did this man become the kind of person who would cheat his own people in their taxes to Rome, even those in his own town, perhaps his close relatives? We might suggest that his short stature played a role. Maybe Zacchaeus felt he got the short end of the stick in life and was due any benefit he could create for himself. Either way, when he heard that Jesus was coming to town, something different came out in Zacchaeus.

There is a child-like aspect to this story that makes it another one readymade for the flannel board. I am sure my Sunday school classroom had a sycamore tree and a Zacchaeus character ready to go. What was it about Jesus, and what was it about Zacchaeus, that prompted him to take this less than dignified action of climbing a tree to see over everyone else's head? Perhaps at the heart of every one of our steps of faith toward Jesus is a prompting from our inner child. Zacchaeus may have been the child who was made fun of, or he was excluded by people his own age. Jesus, of course, would have known that. That would explain Zacchaeus' eager reaction when Jesus made this astonishing request, asking to come to Zacchaeus' own house. Jesus wanted to lift Zacchaeus up in the eyes of those around him who, instead, were used to looking down on him.

The way Jesus phrased his 'request' is also worth considering, *"I must eat at your house today" (Luke 19: 5)*. It is unfortunate that we need to guess at the tone of the voices in the New Testament. If this were written as a novel, the author would have indicated some sort of emotion attached to Jesus' statement or described the look on his face. Was it begrudgingly that Jesus said this? Probably not. Was it sarcastically? I doubt it. Was it ironic, or even with a sense of humor and a broad smile on his face that Jesus made this statement? That makes sense to me. It mirrors Zacchaeus' enthusiasm. In fact, Jesus' enthusiasm might have invited Zacchaeus' ready response. In my imagination, I have always seen Zacchaeus jump out of the tree with a laugh and run home to make the preparations. It is clear that Zacchaeus did not mind the spotlight.

Part of the irony of this story is that Zacchaeus' name means "pure" or "innocent". When Jesus called to him in the tree using Zacchaeus' name, he was stating his value in a positive way to all who were listening. This sets up the dramatic climax of the story when Zacchaeus stood up with great enthusiasm again, proclaiming that he would pay back anyone he cheated, paying them up to four times the amount. All it took for this great reversal in Zacchaeus' life was for someone to show his worth in God's eyes. Some souls are so primed to respond to God that it only takes a hint of good news for their treasure to start to gleam. In response to Zacchaeus' repentance *and* restitution, Jesus made one of his most emphatic statements about the faith of another person. Of Zacchaeus he said: *"Today, salvation has come to this household, for he too is a son of Abraham!" (Luke 19: 9)*. Then Jesus taught the crowd a point of theology: *"For the Son of Man came to seek and save the lost" (Luke 19: 10)*.

Jesus called forth saving faith in Zacchaeus, who had formerly tried to get back at the world through cheating and lying. But instead of exposing Zacchaeus' sin, Jesus exposed his value to God. This is certainly a treasure and a pearl story.

The Woman at the Well in Sychar, (John 4: 1 – 30)

Another situation where Jesus uncovered buried treasure in a person, is the story of his interaction with the Samaritan woman who went to Jacob's well to draw water. Even more than in the case of Zacchaeus, we see Jesus went out of his way for the sake of one person. Breaking tradition, Jesus entered Samaritan lands rather than keeping to the territory of Judea as he made his way back to the Galilee region. In doing so Jesus interacted with a lone Samaritan woman.

This broke the norms of appropriate behavior for a Jewish man on several levels. First, Jews looked down on the Samaritans, who were descended from the ten northern tribes and who, five centuries earlier, had been judged by God for their unfaithfulness. Those who were not killed or dispersed, intermarried with their conquerors. Jews considered the Samaritans of their day to carry the stigma of that unfaithful and mixed heritage.

But even more eyebrow-raising was Jesus' willingness, as a Jewish rabbi, to talk privately with a woman. Contact between Jewish men and women was guarded by many social rules and safeguards. Being alone with a woman who was not related to you through family or marriage, broke these social norms in a big way. Then of course there was the added problem of the woman in this story having such a complicated past. Jesus crossed more than a national boundary to talk with her, he also crossed cultural, religious, and gender barriers. The accumulation of all these norm-breaking activities is seen in the reaction of the disciples when they returned from the market: *"Now at that very moment his disciples came back. They were shocked because he was speaking with a woman"* (John 4: 27a).

But let us back up to the content of Jesus' conversation with her, for it is here that we can appreciate how he uncovered in her a pearl of great price. Jesus chose the well in Sychar as the place he would rest until the disciples returned, knowing that this woman would arrive there. John's account tells us that she was ostracized from her community because of her past, which we might say, mirrored the unfaithfulness of her Samaritan ancestors in Jewish eyes. She had been with five men prior to the man she was now living with. We must guess at the details here, but we can assume she had lived through a string of bad relationships. It is possible that some of these previous men had died, but it is likely that there were many reasons that these relationships ended. Many are quick to assume that she was promiscuous, but that assumption ignores the laws of the day that made marriage the legal domain of men. The text is vague on these past relationships as to whether they were all marriages, and yet Jesus does say that she had five husbands prior to her current relationship. If that is the case, it means that five men had discarded her, giving her a certificate of divorce. But it is also possible that Jesus was just being kind to her, calling her previous men 'husbands'.

Either way, we see her as a woman who had been through a lot, with much that disqualified her, even shamed her, in the eyes of those who strictly followed religious law.

Jesus initiated conversation with her by asking her for a drink from the well. This again crossed a boundary. He was willing to touch something she had touched. He was also putting her into a place of honor by receiving something from her, a sign that he did not reject her. It was Jesus' kindness to her that began to reveal the pearl and the treasure that was hidden below the surface of her wounded life. And yet, we find out right away that she was no fool. She responded to Jesus by challenging him: *"How can you—a Jew—ask me, a Samaritan woman, for water to drink?" (John 4: 8).* In one crisp sentence she names all the improprieties at work here, essentially calling Jesus' bluff. But Jesus was not bluffing. He wanted to recognize her as an intelligent woman, one who could have a theological discussion about worship practices and the historical and religious disagreements between Jews and Samaritans. Jesus allowed and encouraged this meeting of minds.

Most remarkably, Jesus shared with her his vision of the future, the world of the Gospel, the world impacted by his Kingdom. He told her he was preparing a future where there would no longer be divisions among people (such as those between the Jews and the Samaritans), or disagreements about what locations were more sacred for worship (Jerusalem, or Mt. Gerizim). Instead, Jesus told her, *"But a time is coming—and now is here—when the true worshipers will worship the Father in spirit and truth, for the Father seeks such people to be his worshipers. 24 God is spirit, and the people who worship him must worship in spirit and truth" (John 4: 23 – 24).* This is the crux of their conversation, and it is the moment that Jesus turned over the last shovelful of dirt to uncover the treasure in this woman. This Samaritan woman, even with her trail of failed relationships, was among those waiting for the Messiah! *"The woman said, "I know that Messiah"* (called Christ) *"is coming. When he comes, he will explain everything to us" (John 4: 25).*

Beneath all the layers that disqualified her in the eyes of others, there remained this precious pearl of great and profound faith. Jesus used that moment to reveal what he had concealed from so many others, *"I, the one speaking to you, am he" (John 4: 26)*. She believed him! After the disciples returned, this incredible individual — a daughter of Jacob no less — ran back into town to tell everyone about the man who had told her, *"everything I ever did!"* (John 4: 29). They returned with her, and received the good news of Jesus as the Messiah as well.

John's account finishes like this: *"Now many Samaritans from that town believed in him because of the report of the woman who testified, "He told me everything I ever did." ⁴⁰ So when the Samaritans came to him, they began asking him to stay with them. He stayed there two days, ⁴¹ and because of his word many more believed. ⁴² They said to the woman, "No longer do we believe because of your words, for we have heard for ourselves, and we know that this one really is the Savior of the world" (John 4: 39 – 42)*. Few towns over the border in Judea, received, or had faith in, Jesus to such an extent.

The Man in the Gerasene Tombs, (Mark 5: 1 – 17)

The final story of Jesus uncovering a treasure or a pearl in an individual is also the most extreme example of Jesus crossing boundaries for one soul. This time Jesus did not just leave Jewish territory and cross into Samaritan lands, he crossed to the other side of the Sea of Galilee into the region of the Decapolis, the region of the Gentiles. The Decapolis referred to ten cities connected to a former Greek empire. The spiritual darkness of the area is demonstrated immediately. The first person to encounter Jesus was a demonized man who lived in a local cemetery, and who was clearly out of his mind. The local people had tried to chain him to keep him from hurting himself and others, but he just broke those bonds each time. He is presented in Mark's Gospel as a sort of Samson figure, but powered by evil spirits rather than the Spirit of God: *"For his hands and feet had often been bound with chains and shackles, but he had torn the chains apart and broken the shackles in pieces. No one was strong enough to subdue him" (Mark 5: 4).*

There was more going on in this man's life than just a severe case of mental illness. As soon as Jesus got out of the boat, this man came forth from the tombs and mockingly bowed down before him. The spirits that animated him knew who Jesus was: *"When he saw Jesus from a distance, he ran and bowed down before him. [7] Then he cried out with a loud voice, "Leave me alone, Jesus, Son of the Most High God! I implore you by God—do not torment me!" (Mark 5: 6 – 7).* It turned out that there was a legion of demons oppressing this man. But Jesus healed him instantly, sending the spirits amongst a herd of two thousand pigs, that immediately stampeded, and fell over the side of a cliff and tumbled into the sea!

No doubt, this was a dramatic introduction of the ministry of Jesus to the people of the Decapolis. When the locals arrived, they found the man from the tombs sitting with Jesus, clothed and in his right mind. But the disruption was too much for them — probably the destruction of the pigs too — and they asked Jesus to leave. He did, and though the man from the tombs wanted to come with him, Jesus instead instructed him to remain as a lone witness to the coming mission of the Messiah. *"Go to your home and to your people and tell them what the Lord has done for you, that he had mercy on you." [20] So he went away and began to proclaim in the Decapolis what Jesus had done for him, and all were amazed" (Mark 5: 19 – 20).*

The parallels to the story of the Samaritan woman at the well are striking. Jesus crossed boundaries for both individuals, liberated them spiritually, and left them to witness to their communities. Most striking was their success. The woman brought her whole town to faith on the power of her testimony. The man from the tombs brought knowledge of the power of Jesus to his region and people listened in amazement. In all these stories from Jesus' ministry, he surprised people by doing what was out of the ordinary, crossing boundaries and breaking social convention to win one person as part of his treasure on earth. There is a clear mandate here for us as the church today to do the same. We are called to cross boundaries, to break barriers, and to "think outside the box", so that we may uncover many treasures and possess many pearls of great price for the Kingdom of God.

KINGDOM IMPACT EXAMPLE, UNCOVERING HIDDEN VALUE: ST. PAUL BAPTIST, PEORIA, IL — PARTNERSHIP WITH A LOCAL PUBLIC SCHOOL.

Peoria, Illinois, is blessed with a school system that is incredibly open to community partnerships, especially with churches. Kristie Hubbard, a community outreach coordinator on staff at St. Paul Baptist, helped pioneer this movement. She connected her congregation with a local middle school over ten years ago. Kristie served on the Community Foundation Board for the school district that made these partnerships possible. This gave her insight into the way that churches and other organizations were experiencing these partnerships. One thing that Kristie noticed was that middle schools were being passed over. Most churches and other organizations chose elementary schools instead, probably because there is the perception that elementary school kids are easier to work with and that volunteers might be more ready to participate. So intentionally, Kristie guided her congregation to choose a middle school, one located close to the church, Von Steuben Middle School. Her mind was already turning with the possibilities for how God would work.

What is it about middle schoolers that makes some people insecure and even fearful of working with them? It is probably because middle school represents those adolescent years that many of us want to forget. We remember how hard it was to find and maintain friendships in the hyper-competitive social environments of the junior high cafeteria and playground. Most of us can remember being bullied at least once, or perhaps many times. It is also a time of physical awkwardness; many of us became very self-conscious, suddenly concerned for our daily appearance and how we were judged by our peers.

That is why this story is a wonderful example of a church intentionally throwing its arms around a group that some might choose to pass by. With Kristie's guidance, St. Paul Baptist looked at the field, represented by Von Steuben, and said: "I see hidden treasure there. That is a pearl of great price." Middle schoolers are going through one of the most significant mental changes in human development. During those awkward years, their brains are moving from a base of concrete thinking to the ability to make symbolic connections. Ministry to adolescents needs to change dramatically after young people make that shift. The Gospel can be taught in rich and creative ways when the important metaphorical connections can be understood, when the images of shepherd, king, savior, perfect sacrifice, and many more, can be appreciated for all their rich meaning. While a younger child will understand a parable as a story that teaches a lesson, an adolescent can understand it as a story that reveals how God wants to relate to them personally. Adolescence is a time of necessary re-evangelization, when the Gospel of Jesus can, and needs to, make sense on this symbolic level so it may become a life-long faith. It is why so many researchers have indicated that unless a young person comes to personal faith by age fourteen, with every passing year after that, it becomes increasingly unlikely that they ever will, (Kennedy, The 4–14 Window; Steve S Chang, Don't Neglect the 4–14 Window).

Early on in the partnership, St. Paul Baptist focused on giving financial support to the school, purchasing uniforms for kids whose families did not have the funds to cover them, or helping the school buy specialized learning software. Volunteers began serving as lunchroom monitors who provided familiar and consistent faces. They were able to build relationships with students on a different level than a teacher or other staff member could. It makes a difference to have a whole other set of caring adults who do not have educational responsibilities or hold power in any other way. These volunteers were simply able to engage in an emotionally supportive way, searching out kids who looked stressed, sad, or anxious.

Each year, Kristie contacted the school to find out what was specifically needed in coming semesters. She found that these needs changed often, especially when the school transitioned through different administrators. But each year, the approach has been to let the school and the students drive the relationship.

A few years into this partnership, St. Paul Baptist decided to go the next step by providing a tutoring ministry in their church building for Von Steuben kids needing extra help. Kristie arranged for drivers from the church to pick up kids following afternoon activities a couple days a week. This was a critical juncture. They learned that many kids were unsupervised between the time school ended and when parents made it home from work. This was an ideal moment to fill a need that was previously unseen. St. Paul provided adults who were background-checked and able to give educational support. The school advertised this option to the students and their families, and soon 8 – 10 students were making use of this opportunity. As the partnership developed, St. Paul also made some of its other ministries, a Scout troop and a ministry helping girls with self-esteem, available to these students as well.

This is where relational ministry really moved to a new level. Tutoring the students in the church building allowed more freedom for adults to provide emotional and spiritual help along with the educational support. While Kristie hesitates to call this true mentoring because the adults and students do not meet outside these proscribed times, it was clear that students were being cared for in a church environment in a different way than they were during school lunch hours. As the students got to know the adults better, they began to share more about their needs and concerns. Soon an organization affiliated with Caterpillar Inc, the Caterpillar African American Network, partnered directly with St. Paul Baptist, sending employees with math and science backgrounds to help the students with difficult coursework in a more profound way. Many of the students at Von Steuben are of African American or another minority background. These professionals were able to model a career path for minority students in a tangible and personal way.

Kristie pointed out that several students they have served have gone on to excel in high school and college, in part because of the consistent support that the members and partners of St. Paul Baptist have provided. While it is not always seen immediately in adolescents, these kinds of supportive and mentoring relationships pay dividends and call out value and worth in the lives of young people that might have otherwise missed out on the opportunity. A few students have contacted St. Paul to give this ministry credit for helping them reach their goals. There have been several cases where families have clearly indicated the value of the church's support. One family said this to Kristie and other leaders in the ministry about their son who had previously been getting into trouble: "His life changed as a result of having someone else checking in with him and following up."

Kristie Hubbard put it this way: "God's hand is really at work in every part of this. Our congregation's goal is to 'live and love like Christ'". God shows up all the time because we seek to "do life together". When you see a child overcome his or her struggles with algebra and you can say: "Hey, God helped you do that!" you are connecting faith and life in a real way.

Discussion Questions:

1. What aspects of the story of St. Paul Baptist's relationship with the local middle school was most inspiring for you?
2. When you think of the youth in your community, what groups do you see as 'passed over' or ignored?
3. Which of the two interpretations of the Parables of the Treasure and the Pearl of Great Price speak more powerfully to you and why?
4. If you are honest, what values drive your church in its decision-making?
5. When have you seen the church embrace a new person in such a way as to bring out the hidden treasure in them, the treasure that God has always seen?
6. Where do you see negative labeling as holding back potential Kingdom Impact in your community?

CHAPTER 6

The Parable of the Net —
Casting a Broad Net

*"Once again, the kingdom of heaven is like a net that
was let down into the lake and caught all kinds of fish.
⁴⁸ When it was full, the fishermen pulled it up on the
shore. Then they sat down and collected the good fish
in baskets, but threw the bad away. ⁴⁹ This is how it
will be at the end of the age. The angels will come and
separate the wicked from the righteous ⁵⁰ and throw
them into the blazing furnace, where there will be
weeping and gnashing of teeth."*

Matthew 13: 47 – 50

I have had the chance to work with commercial fishermen,
harvesting fish from their herring nets. In their retirement, my
grandparents settled on an island in Lunenburg County, Nova
Scotia. When I visited them each summer, I looked forward to the
morning when I got to accompany the fishermen, steaming three

miles out into the North Atlantic to their herring nets. I recall those cool, dark mornings fondly; the rise and fall of the deck of the cape islander fishing vessel under my feet was just what a suburban kid needed to broaden his horizons. When the sun rose, it illuminated the surface of the ocean and revealed fishing boats of all sizes and colors that had been waiting there in the dark. Like protecting angels, flocks of seagulls filled the air above each vessel. The horizon seemed limitless.

The men I worked with those summer days made their living from the sea in the same manner as the fishermen Jesus knew. Fishermen are men of faith. Their entire livelihood is based on their ability to envision the fish they seek, hiding somewhere beneath the surface, invisible, but real in their mind's eye. It is the persistent faith of a fisherman that compels him to return day after day, to cast his nets again, wait, and pray. Little silver herring were the stock and trade of the men I worked with, but often there were other fish that also found their way into the gill nets. Occasionally we were lucky enough to catch a few codfish or haddock along with the herring. But in most cases the extra fish were really ugly: hake, sculpins and dogfish. The dogfish were the worst. Being miniature sharks, just three feet in length, they tore up the nets with their muscular bodies as they thrashed around to get free.

One morning, we found that an entire net was filled with them; hundreds of dogfish were caught where herring should have been. The captain explained what we had to do. Each shark had to be removed carefully without further damaging the net. This was delicate work as the dogfish had razor sharp teeth and a sharp spine just behind their dorsal fin that carried a mild sting. Then, as though in an act of judgment, each shark had to be killed. Holding their tails, we were instructed to raise the dogfish over our heads and bringing their backbone down hard against the gunwale of the boat, breaking their spine. This gruesome task having been accomplished, we could let loose our grip, allowing them to slip away into the dark deep. This is how we sorted the good fish from the bad.

It was a gruesome task that still brings shivers to my own spine when I think of it. I did not want to carry out the task. But I knew that these men were trusting us to follow their orders. The dogfish could destroy tens of thousands of dollars of vital equipment. I admit that I let many of them go when the captain's back was turned.

This last Kingdom parable of Matthew 13 is an eschatological one. This is a theological term meaning "having to do with the end." The end, in this case, is the end of time, the end of the age, the time of God's judgment on humanity. There are parables I enjoy more. I do not want to think about people gnashing their teeth in agony and in bitter regret over what could have been for them had they not resisted the goodness and grace of God when it was so abundantly free. None of us can really imagine what it would be like for the goodness and grace of God to be suddenly absent from creation. Right now, we are immersed in it; we swim through it just as fish move through the ocean. In the same way, we hardly notice the air around us, though it sustains our lives moment by moment.

Fish have no idea what it is like to be out of the water, that is, until they are. And when you have a fish out of water you can see the panic, the gasping, and the frantic attempt to find it again. That is a good image for what it will be like one day for the person who rejects the Gospel when the grace of God is removed from creation. When that happens, all that will remain will be the stark reality of judgment. The writer of the letter to the Hebrews put it this way: *"If we deliberately keep on sinning after we have received the knowledge of the truth, no sacrifice for sins is left, ²⁷ but only a fearful expectation of judgment and of raging fire that will consume the enemies of God"* (Hebrews 10: 27).

But for those who have gladly and gratefully received the mercy of God, the undeserved merit of Christ imparted by faith, they will find that they have already passed from judgment into grace, from death into life. Jesus' own words confirm this: *"Very truly I tell you, whoever hears my word and believes him who sent me has eternal life and will not be judged but has crossed over from death to life"* (John 5: 24).

For those who have accepted Christ and received the grace associated with his sacrificial act on the cross, when the time of the judgement comes, they will not feel like a fish out of water. But for those who have knowingly rejected Christ and his mercy, there will be the anticipation of accountability before God: *"And I saw the dead, great and small, standing before the throne, and books were opened. Another book was opened, which is the book of life. The dead were judged according to what they had done as recorded in the books"* (Revelation 20:12). It will be a terrifying thing to stand before the Judgement Seat on the final day without the protecting grace of Jesus. I am sure it will feel like you cannot breathe.

I do not want to picture anyone in that situation. I am thankful that God's grace has found me. I am thankful for my own salvation. But my awareness of God's plan does not let me simply sit in my own spiritual comfort and peace. God has called us into partnership with him in the renewal of all creation, which includes the calling of men and women into relationship with the Lord of life and love. The prophet Isaiah felt this urgency even for the people of his day, seven hundred years before Jesus' birth: *"Seek the LORD while he may be found; call on him while he is near"* (Isaiah 55:6). I love that this passage is found in the Old Testament. The grace and mercy of God were at work in those days too, hidden in the Old Covenant that became the foundation of the New Covenant we enjoy in the age of the Gospel. Jesus is reigning at the right hand of the Father. We claim this truth each time we say the Apostles' Creed, which itself says: "He [Jesus] ascended into heaven and is seated at the right hand of the Father. He will come again to judge the living and the dead." This is the Apostolic teaching which the early church affirmed and clung to, as it says in Acts 2: 42. We still claim it today.

As we finish this study of Kingdom Impact, and what Jesus' Kingdom parables say about making that impact, we need to wrestle with the meaning of this final parable. What mandate does it present from Jesus to the Church today? The answer: It has to do with the net. In whose hands *is* the net? The parable tells us it is the fishermen who hold it, and it is the fishermen who let it down into the water to bring up the fish. Jesus was clear at the calling of the disciples that he would make them fishers of men. He did not change their profession, just their object of their search. That net is in the hands of your church. It is in your hands and it is in mine. We are in the boat which is meant to catch people for the Kingdom of God.

The image of the church as a boat is an ancient one. For the early Christians, it reminded them of the ark of Noah in which humanity was rescued from an earlier judgement. Many church sanctuaries throughout the ages were constructed with great soaring wooden ribs coming together at the pinnacle of a curved roof. This was understood originally to be an upturned hull. Unawares, many Christians today worship each week under the upturned hull of a ship — God's rescue boat for humanity. But so few of us get our hands wet by handling a net or fish that it is easy to forget that fact. In fact, many churches have been transformed into cruise liners, fitted with comfortable cabins, restaurants, movie theaters, and lots of entertainment. There is even a staff available that will take care of everyone's needs. Ouch! The 'passengers' on a cruise liner can be at sea for weeks and not once come into contact with the ocean itself, let alone any fish — unless it is served to them at dinner! They have paid to be there after all; other people are doing the work.

This image of the church as a cruise ship is painfully familiar today. Let us be clear, it has nothing to do with the working boats that Jesus had in mind in this parable, or the nets he has placed into our hands. Jesus calls his Church to the task of the Kingdom. We are his Body on earth, his hands and feet, the fulfillment of his sufferings and the continuation of his ministry. The night before he was led to the cross, he told his disciples, *"You are those who have stood by me in my trials. 29 And I confer on you a kingdom, just as my Father conferred one on me, 30 so that you may eat and drink at my table in my kingdom and sit on thrones, judging the twelve tribes of Israel"* *(Luke 22: 28b – 30).* Jesus has an amazing future role in mind for those who believe and follow him!

So, what is the net, then? What is actually in our hands? It is the mandate to create a crowd that the Spirit of God will sift and sort by way of the Gospel. The Church is in the business of calling and gathering people together for the hearing of God's Word. That sounds like church worship, and it certainly is. That is certainly one kind of net. But have you noticed that it is mostly *churched* people who come to church on a Sunday morning? There are many more people who might not come for a worship service but will come and be part of a crowd for lots of other reasons. That is where we must get creative.

We could exhaust the rest of the pages of this book listing all the manners in which churches create crowds. That would not help us any further down the road. We need to create the kinds of crowds that are suited to our own neighborhoods and communities. One of the interesting things about commercial fishing nets is they are colored differently for different kinds of water. In some cases, it is a blue or greenish net that will be invisible to fish because that is the color of the water as refracted light travels down from the surface. In other bodies of water, the net must be brown or yellow to be invisible. This is a reminder that what works for one church and for one community will not work for all.

When churches create crowds for an event, most often those crowds are not truly diverse. Most churches create crowds of people who look and think like the people who are already in that church. They like the same kind of music, have the same level of education, vote the same way, and have a similar worldview. The net that Jesus talked about in this parable is very different. It captures all kinds of fish, both "good" and "bad". The net is wide and broad and necessitates a sorting of the fish. The kinds of crowds most churches gather do not require much sorting.

In the Parable of the Net, it is the angels of God that do the sorting of the fish. When we present the Gospel to people, God is working behind the scenes to reinforce and to push that Word deep in ways that only he knows how to do for each person. I have heard people refer to a preacher or Christian speaker, saying: "It was like they were talking just to me!" *That is the sorting happening in real time.* I have had people come to me after worship on a Sunday and tell me what they heard in the message that morning, and yet, it was different from what I actually said. At times I have wondered if they were listening to a podcast instead! *But that is the sorting happening in real time.* Our job is to get people there, a diverse crowd of believers and unbelievers, old and young, healthy and wounded, good and bad. We are called to preach the Gospel and then to trust in the work of the Spirit of God, and, according to Jesus, trust the angels of God who are his messengers, to sort it all out and apply the Word.

When my current congregation began to minister to a local neighborhood, we suddenly had lots of folks interacting with our church who were new to the church 'thing'. This was hard for some of our church members. They did not necessarily know what to do with all these new fish. It took time to sort it out. Some of the new folks have stayed and have grown in Christ, their treasure revealed. Man, do we have some pearls! But others seemed repelled by the message and moved on. I can only interpret that in one way: *the sorting was playing out in real time.* As I watch this process happen over and over, I am reminded of the number of times in my life that I was the one who walked away. But God did not give up on me; nor did his church. We must continue to cast a broad net, and return, just like a fisherman, to do it again and again. I am convinced it is God's will that we do so, otherwise we risk being the fishing boat that has decided instead to be a cruise ship, with all the amenities for the paying customers. I want to make sure we are continuing to get our hands wet and scaly and that we remember to cast the net out again, even on the other side of the boat this time.

As we said at the beginning of this chapter, the stakes in this case are high. This is a matter of spiritual life and spiritual death. Jesus has conferred upon us his Kingdom. We have got to take that responsibility seriously. As Jesus says in another parable outside Matthew 13, God wants his banquet hall full, and he will go into the countryside to fill seats if he needs to.

Kingdom Impact Example, Casting a Broad Net: Living Waters Church — The Father / Daughter Dance.

One of the surprising stories of ministry at my current congregation is the Father / Daughter Dance. Living Waters did not set out to have a ministry that was potentially city-wide. It was a vision that started in the way that so many of Jesus' Kingdom parables start — small. A father and daughter in our congregation had enjoyed going to a special dance for daddies and daughters held in a community about an hour away. When that event was discontinued, the girl, Sophie, who was in middle school at that point, continued to ask her father, Allen, if they were going to go to another Father / Daughter Dance? Eventually Allen asked Sophie what she thought about our church hosting a dance instead? This little conversation was just the kind of seed that Jesus talked about. It was an idea that would catch on and shelter many. It was a seed that was going to be planted in soil that must have been uniquely prepared, because such an idea would not work in every town or every place. Together Sophie and Allen, along with Allen's wife Pam, put together the vision for what would become our Father / Daughter dance. The goal was to create a simple evening, just a place for dads and daughters to be together to celebrate that unique and powerful relationship that God uses to grow healthy, confident young ladies.

Roughly 150 people came in the first year, in 2011, representing about 60 families. Ninety-five percent of those in attendance were from the community. There was a DJ playing both clean secular and Christian dance songs in the gym, and a punch fountain and ice cream sundaes in a side room. One of the most touching elements of the evening was a special room where dads and daughters could have a professional photo taken and another room where daughters could assemble a stuffed animal with a pocket into which dads could put a note to their daughters on a red paper heart.

We thought 150 participants was an amazing number for a congregation that was about 100 – 120 people at that time. It was wonderful to see these men dressed in their best suits and their girls, ages one to eighteen, wearing prom dresses, dancing, and laughing. Allen was overwhelmed with many emails from dads expressing their thanks and indicating their surprise that such an event would be offered for free. But that was part of the vision. We wanted to create a crowd. Allen and Pam, however, had a vision for an even larger crowd, and so did God. Allen felt called to have men from all over the city come, fathers and uncles, grandfathers, and family friends.

Word of mouth spread the news; Allen used connections he had through Boy Scouts and other organizations, and ads were created for Christian and secular radio. The following year the dance doubled in size. The next year it doubled again, and the following year it grew as well. By the sixth year we hit a high of over 800 participants (father, daughters, and volunteers) and we were forced to use almost every room in the building. With the event being that size, the decision was made to move it to a local Christian school. Part of the understanding here was that while Living Waters was sponsoring the dance, we knew this was God's event and the goal was to bless the families of Peoria. The location did not matter as Living Waters was now partnering with many local businesses and restaurants to cover costs and supply door prizes and gifts. A special feature of the evening, chosen by many of the fathers at that point, was to take their daughters out for dinner before the dance. Some restaurants in town were now offering discounts for dance participants.

One of the things this event has taught us is the very theme we are exploring — impact versus growth. Not one new family or individual has become part of Living Waters because of the dance. Not one. The first couple of years we wondered about that. We had seen the event as an effort of our evangelism team, of which Allen was the leader. How could we call this evangelism if our congregation was not growing as a result? But that seemed to be the lesson that God was teaching us. Evangelism is not about growing your own congregation, although that can be a blessing and a side effect. The emails that Allen continued to receive expressing their heartfelt thanks, communicated plenty about the value of the dance as an outreach. Here are examples of some emails that Allen has received over the years:

> *"Thank you very much, Allen. We absolutely love the event! Thank you for being such a blessing to so many families and for the memories you help us make. Sincerely, Olga."*

> *"Thank you so much!!! My daughter went last year for the first time and it was such a highlight of her year and she has talked about it probably daily since... She sleeps with her stuffed animal from last year every single night... Thanks again!! Mindy"*

> *"Thank you Allen. It was a great time again. Even better this year than last. My daughter was on cloud 9. Sincerely, Sean."*

There is one response that remains close to Allen's heart. He received an email from the mother of a girl who had been coming for three years with her father. In the previous year, however, her dad suddenly died. She asked if Allen had any pictures still on file from previous dances. She explained that her daughter had one photo that was taken of her and her dad dancing and that it was always at her bedside. The mother concluded the email with this: *"You are creating great memories for girls by setting the right example for them to learn how to be treated as they grow older and get into relationships, and for them to see how God sees them as special, precious, princesses, Sandra."*

We have concluded that God is doing much more with this crowd than growing the membership of one church. Instead, God is allowing one little congregation to serve a city of fathers and daughters and to encourage a healthy and positive relationship that we are convinced is life-changing for both. Some of my best memories are the years I have taken my own daughters. Each year God is honored in prayer, a short devotion is offered. Everyone knows a church hosts the event. In fact, this is the one thing our congregation is known for in the community. If I say, "I am the pastor of Living Waters," people often say, "Oh the father/daughter dance church! My (husband / uncle / son) goes to that. It's really great." I get to say, "Thank you, I'm really glad to hear that they are part of the crowd."

We have not received one new member, but members of churches all over the city, as well as men who do not attend church (and a few that attend a mosque, temple, or synagogue) are being blessed and receiving the message that Jesus cares about something as foundational as the relationship they share with their daughters. Praise God for that.

Every year, several men express their desire to pay for something. They are overwhelmed again that such an evening would be free. So, now we give them something to pay for. Each family receives a little packet of the mission partners we support and a fundraising goal we have for a mission trip or service project. We let them pay for that. Again, a little taste of the Kingdom of God, a little chance to participate in the impact of that Kingdom.

Discussion Questions:

1. What aspects of the story of Living Waters' Father/Daughter Dance were surprising, challenging or encouraging to you?
2. How do you understand the message of the Parable of the Net differently having read this chapter?
3. What do you think it means to cast a broad or wide net?
4. Have you witnessed the kind of "sorting" described in this chapter?
5. Having read this, do you have any ideas of how your congregation may create just such a crowd in which the Spirit of God might do his work?

CHAPTER 7:

Forward Toward Kingdom Impact
— A Seventh Kingdom Parable?

"He said to them, "Therefore every teacher of the law
who has become a disciple in the kingdom of heaven
is like the owner of a house who brings out of his
storeroom new treasures as well as old."

Matthew 13: 52

I like to refer to this passage at the end of Jesus' Kingdom parables as the forgotten parable of Matthew 13. Jesus concludes his Kingdom parables with this final formidable metaphor, a cryptic message that is as layered as an onion. It involves a teacher, a disciple, a homeowner, a storeroom, and new and old treasures. Are you following? This is easily the most complicated parable in the New Testament, and yet, Jesus offers no explanation to help us decipher it. This is the conclusion to the sermon he presented to those gathered by the lake, and later, to those who accompanied him to the house as referenced in Matthew 13: 36. That house, we can assume, is the home that served as Jesus' center of operations in Capernaum in the early stages of his ministry. It was there that Jesus asked his followers: *"Have you understood these things?"* The group gathered in the house answered, *"Yes" (Matthew 13: 51).* Previously, Jesus had given them six lenses through which to see and perceive the work of the Kingdom in the world. But then, surprisingly, he presented one more. He proceeded to test their understanding by way of this seventh parable. So, do you understand what he is saying?

Let me set the stage. Southdale Center in Edina, Minnesota, was built in 1956 as the first indoor shopping mall in America. That is fitting for a state where it is really only safe to be outside six months of the year. I say this as someone who lived in the Twin Cities area for fifteen years. Southdale offered this climate-controlled environment in which to service your shopping habit, out of the wind, snow, and freezing temperatures. No longer was there a need to put on your boots and stocking cap, and zip up your jacket to go from store to store. Just waltz from place to place, get a coffee, you know... spend the day. What a revolution! Every mall in America can trace its DNA back to Southdale's central rotunda with all its fancy escalators.

Fast forward fifty years and you have Mall of America, the same metropolitan area, built for the same reasons, but for a whole new time. An old idea, reborn. Mall of America is the largest mall in the United States, owned by the same company that built the West Edmonton Mall, which is the largest indoor mall in the world. Forty million people visit Mall of America each year; that is the entire population of Canada. The statistics listed on the website of Mall of America indicate it would take eighty-six hours to visit each store, if you remained in each one for only ten minutes. It is a half-mile walk around just one level; there are four floors of retail heaven. Imagine four retail-ladened 'donuts' stacked on top of one another — that is the Mall of America. Then, when you have made around all four levels, there is an amusement park inside the donut hole, with roller coasters and water rides to enjoy.

What does this have to do with Jesus' final parable in Matthew

13? The story of the oldest and largest malls in the United States is just something old repackaged and upgraded to be something new. Is that what Jesus is talking about in this little parable? Let us review it: *"He said to them, "Therefore every teacher of the law who has become a disciple in the kingdom of heaven is like the owner of a house who brings out of his storeroom new treasures as well as old" (Matthew 13: 52).*

Let us start with the word "therefore". Each time you see the word "therefore" in the Bible you must assume that the speaker is making a conclusion based on what has been previously presented. After the previous six parables, Jesus gives us this scenario: A teacher of the law (a Pharisee or a Sadducee) becomes a disciple in the kingdom of heaven. Whoa, let us back up the train! The teachers of the law were Jesus' main opponents. They were the ones who constantly challenged him in his teaching and his behavior. They repeatedly accused him of breaking God's law, tried to test him in his teaching, and tried to trip him up and catch him being inconsistent in his words. They never did. And yet, that is how Jesus began his conclusion to the Kingdom parables: with one of the arch enemies of Jesus' movement becoming a follower instead of an opponent. A teacher of the Old Covenant with its laws and regulations, becomes a teacher of the New Covenant instead, and a participant and a disciple in the Kingdom of God.

We cannot just skip over this. Jesus is doing something revolutionary here. He is saying that the vision of the Kingdom of Heaven is not something new. In fact, it was hidden in all that God had done with his chosen people since the time of the covenant he made with Abraham. God is a covenant maker. God, in his faithfulness, does not exchange one promise for another, as though the promises of the Old Covenant are now obsolete and replaced by new promises. Instead, these are promises built on promises. The idea Jesus presents here is that the people of Jesus' own generation would move from the Old Covenant to the New Covenant, following — do not miss this — following their *own* teachers as they, themselves, discover what God is doing!

Jesus is putting on his rabbi hat here. He is the first of many rabbis who would become a teacher of the New Covenant, planting the seed and unearthing the treasure of what God is doing in the long game. Who is best suited to understand that God's new work is a fulfillment of his original work, the fulfillment of all his ancient promises? Answer: one who has known and taught the old law faithfully and with understanding, one who had now been released into the freedom of God's Kingdom in Jesus Christ. Does anyone come to mind here? Can anyone say the Apostle Paul? What about Nicodemus who came to Jesus at night seeking greater understanding, wanting to know more? Along with the crowds, it was these teachers that Jesus really wanted to capture, the ones with whom he stood toe-to-toe in the marketplace and the synagogue. Both John 12: 42 and Acts 6:7 suggest that many of the priests became believers in Jesus. How many Jewish religious leaders became followers of Jesus' New Covenant? We do not know. But imagine the powerful witness of those who did. The Pharisees were Jesus' greatest opponents, but they could be even greater evangelists for God's New Way.

Let us move forward. What would it mean for a teacher of the law, one who had been an expert in God's Old Covenant promises, to receive the Gospel and to become a joyful preacher of God's Kingdom in Christ? Such a person would have come to the personal conviction that what God was doing first with his chosen people, Israel, he now wanted to do with all nations and all peoples. This hypothetical teacher of God's new law in Christ would have passion to bring all people into God's loving favor and mercy, so they might share the new inheritance of eternal life. The righteousness that the law required had been fulfilled in the death and resurrection of Jesus. This teacher of the law would see that Jesus *is* the New Covenant as well as the Old Covenant fulfilled, and that God's grace was now available and open — just like the man in Luke 14, who threw open the doors of his banquet hall to all who would come. God wants his house full.

This is what a teacher of the law who became a Gospel preacher would understand. And what does Jesus say about such a person? Get ready for the meaning of the last Kingdom parable in Matthew 13: *"They are like the owner of a house who brings out of his storeroom new treasures as well as old"* (verse 52). Cue the crickets... Okay. Wait, Jesus, is that it? I would have expected instead a thunderclap to accompany the great reveal. But, instead, Jesus is being very subtle. Rather than finishing these parables with an exclamation mark, Jesus finishes with a dot, dot, dot. I want to suggest a few things to help us understand what is going on.

First, Jesus is teaching all this in advance of his death and resurrection. He is foreshadowing what will be accomplished at the end of his earthly ministry. In terms of Matthew's Gospel, we are not even halfway through its twenty-eight chapters. The people to whom Jesus was speaking were still living under the Old Covenant. That year, the temple sacrifices would continue. The cross was still on the horizon.

Let us understand, the Kingdom had begun with Jesus' ministry. But it was more like the new king had been born before the old king had died. Jesus was still in the process of making the way for his Kingdom to come to the world, and he had yet to accomplish his sacrificial work on the cross. The New Covenant, the New Creation, and the new reality represented by the Kingdom parables, were going to cost Jesus something, his *everything*, just as The Parables of the Treasure and the Pearl explained. But for those who were listening to what Jesus taught, they were having their first taste of what would soon be the new 'law of the land'. It was as though they were sitting on the bridge between an old and new country.

We can relate to that as Christians today. We also live in an in-between time. We are New Covenant people; we are part of the New Creation of God; it has begun in us. But it has not yet fully come to the world. We *do* live in what is the Kingdom of God today, with free access to God's grace through Christ. But we also live in expectation of what will one day be — God's full and glorious future, revealed for the world, when Jesus returns to receive his Bride, the Church, those who have placed their faith in him. Like the disciples in Matthew 13, we live in the dot, dot, dot, too. We are waiting for the end of the sentence, and for God to begin the new sentence of eternity. Jesus finished this chapter of parables on this subtle note because the Kingdom he was building was still under construction. The cross, which is the bridge from the old to the new, had yet to be put in place. Jesus had yet to build the bridge to life.

In the context to this final parable in Mathew 13, we have covered the meaning of the teacher and the disciple. But what is the storeroom, and who is the homeowner? We know who is the homeowner from Jesus' description: That is any disciple of Jesus who is already a minister of the New Covenant. But the parable hinges now on what they are going to *do*. So does every parable in this chapter, in fact! The man had to *plant* the seed in good soil; the owner of the field had to *decide* what to do about the weeds; the mustard seed needed *planting*; the yeast had to be *mixed* into the dough; the field and the pearl had to be *purchased*; and the net had to be *unfurled* and *cast* into the sea. Every parable of the Kingdom necessitates action, so does this final one. It is this: The minister of the Gospel must learn how to bring out of the storehouse both old and new treasures. The storehouse is the Word of God, which contains the Old and the New Covenants, in perfect relationship: the "old", being, the foundation of God's promises, the "new", being, the fulfillment of all that God has ever promised. The Bible tells us that all God's promises are answered in Christ, with an enthusiastic "Yes!" (2 Corinthians 1: 20).

What is the implication for you and me as part of the Church today, and as part of the community in which your church is planted? We are called to preach Christ and the new hope offered in him, upon the foundation of all that God had done to prepare the soil. We are called to present this full revelation of God to the world, as ministers of the New Covenant who also understand the Old Covenant. That understanding is needed to appreciate what the New Covenant cost God. It is not just me who is called to do this, as one who carries around a diploma from a religious institution and a certificate of ordination. You are a Gospel minister in full standing in the Kingdom of God!

The purpose of this book has been to help you, as a minister of the New Covenant, to look at your church through a new lens — really, six new lenses — each provided by Jesus himself. I have been doing that too. It is the reason I began writing in the first place. I did not begin to write because I am an expert in making Kingdom Impact. But I am a learner and a follower, and I want to understand directly from Jesus how to help my congregation do more effective outreach his way. Jesus is the expert on making Kingdom Impact.

In Matthew 13, we were given six measuring sticks to help us assess the effectiveness of our congregations in making impact in the world. Often when we think about Kingdom Impact, we think just about evangelism. We get scared and feel guilty; finally, we become ineffective. We get stuck because we have this unfocused image, a blurry vision of what the impact of the Kingdom really means, and we become intimidated by it. But now imagine, instead, that Jesus' Kingdom parables in Matthew 13 are like that remarkable device your optometrist swings in front of your face, the one that looks like a set of binoculars for an elephant. You are asked to look through that device at the word chart on the opposite wall. Then, one by one, the optometrist flips a series of lenses over your eyes to correct what you see. With each new lens, the image improves. As he flips the lenses, my optometrist says, "How does that look?... How about now?... And, now?" That is how these parables can work for any church leader, any ministry leader, or any church member, who wants to begin to make greater Kingdom Impact. At some point you are going to say, "There, that's clear. I see it."

Make the commitment to think about at least one of the lenses Jesus has given you in his Word. It is a tool to both measure and calibrate one aspect of your congregation's outreach into the world. In summary, ask these questions:

- Is my congregation looking for good soil to identify the most receptive and open place to scatter the seed of God's

Word? Or are we just throwing it everywhere hoping it will find some good soil?

- Are we confronting the effects of evil in our community? Or are we just ignoring it, hoping it will just go away and stop its insidious work?
- Where could we invest in a small mission partner and help that organization take a big step forward to make outsized-impact for God's mission?
- Are we working to bring about cultural change in our community in a way that honors and reveals Kingdom values? If not, what exciting transformation could be initiated?
- Are there people nearby, maybe even connected to our congregation already, in whom we might uncover a treasure and help them see their value to God and to others?
- And finally, in what new ways could we cast a wide net and pull many people together into a crowd where God's Word might do its saving work?

I promise you, even if you help your church to do just one of these impactful actions you will be building the Kingdom of God in a new, exciting, and meaningful way. It will be Jesus' work done through you and your congregation. You will have taken that initial step to help your congregation be a church on mission in your community, to make Kingdom Impact there on your corner. Most importantly, you will *turn* a corner. You will be partnering with Jesus himself to bring about the renewal of all things. We will finish with this closing thought, stated by many church leaders: The local church is God's "Plan A" for the salvation of the world and the renewal of all creation. There is no "Plan B."

God bless you, *Plan A*.

Discussion Questions:

1. Which 'lens' associated with Jesus' Matthew 13 parables is most important for your congregation right now to evaluate its impact?

2. Which 'lens' has helped you see your community through new eyes?

3. With what key leader will you share your discernment in this area?

4. What research can you do in your community to better understand how your church could make Kingdom Impact?

5. What resistance do you imagine you will find in your congregation to these ideas?

6. All the examples of churches making Kingdom Impact in this book have been from one small geographic area. That was intentional. It demonstrates how powerfully God is at work through local congregations everywhere. How well do you know what God is doing through various churches in your city, town, or area? What is the spiritual landscape like where you live? How could you find out, and how could your congregation join that landscape in an impactful way by doing what other congregations are not?

7. How committed are you to seeing your congregation become a team for making Kingdom Impact in the world?

EPILOGUE: BECOMING A TEAM
FOR KINGDOM IMPACT
(Training Resource)

One of the radical implications of the mission mandates found in Jesus' Kingdom parables, is that congregations must become Kingdom Impact teams. This is counter to the average churchgoer's understanding of what church is all about. For many, if not most, church is the place that you go to get your spiritual needs met. This can be as disconnected as seeing church as the place for weddings, funerals, and baptisms, as well as the odd Christmas Eve or Easter Sunday service with extended family. But a regular church member, active most weeks in Sunday morning worship and midweek activities such as Bible study or small groups, may still have that mindset that church is the place he or she goes to get 'fed' or to 'connect' with God.

One of the shifts I suggested early on, was moving from a Church Growth mentality to a Kingdom Impact mentality. While this is not always the case, Church Growth models tend to imply getting more people into the pews to consume inspirational Christian content from Christian professionals. If a congregation becomes oriented toward Kingdom Impact, the mindset instead becomes one of shared mission, seeing the local congregation as mobilized to bring Gospel transformation to the community outside its walls. We have looked to Jesus' six Kingdom parables for guidance on how to do that effectively.

However, the shift from an interior focus to an exterior focus is, by no means, an easy one; especially, since it can cause confusion amongst long-term members who are not fully on board with the shift. Leaders can experience pushback as people become fearful that those who are already part of the church might now "matter less". This "what about us?" resistance must be anticipated by the leadership from the beginning, or the shift will be extremely difficult and could even fail, resulting in a church collapsing back in upon itself. The key is to address these fears Biblically and understand them as natural and *legitimate* questions that will further clarify the mission of the church to the world.

The truth is you need both in-reach and out-reach to have a healthy church. Not all the energy and passion can go outward. There must be a healthy and robust inner life to a congregation for potential new folks to discover and join. Becoming a church that makes Kingdom Impact effectively will attract attention. People will naturally want to come and see what is going on when they are positively impacted by a church living out Jesus' Kingdom in their community. They will come with respect and buy-in for the mission of the church, even prior to worshipping or joining a small group or Bible study. They will come with a testimony of how that congregation demonstrated care in their lives and in the lives of others they know and love. These are missionaries and ministers in the making. They have already been assimilated into the impact-vision of the congregation. They represent the new culture the leaders are wanting to foster.

But if they come and find a church that is empty of internal life and vitality, or is rife with internal conflict and stresses, they will feel disoriented and discouraged. The church they perceived from the outside was not the church the discovered on the inside. This will be devastating to a person who might be completely new to the Gospel and new to the mission of Jesus. It might be enough to turn them away, and all that impact will be lost.

That is why the members of the church, who react to a Kingdom

Impact approach with suspicion, must be affirmed in their concerns that the inner life of the church will remain strong, and that the existing membership will not be neglected. They are right about those concerns. But where they need to be discipled is that the church was never about "them" in the first place. Healthy members are always those who are connected to the mission of Jesus to bring the outsider in, to seek and save the lost, and to bring healing to the world. Jesus left the ninety-nine to seek the one, but he returned the lost one to the flock. The church has that dual mission: the congregation's creative and vibrant impact on the community for the Kingdom of God, as well as the inner health and vibrancy of the congregation. In a healthy church, one will become an expression of the other.

Of course, this book focuses on just one side of the equation: to shed light on the external call, using Jesus' own words in Matthew 13. There are many great resources already in print related to healthy internal ministries and the inner life of the church. Our purpose here is not to try to reproduce that. But the truth is, you will never join Jesus in his Kingdom mission to your community if you do not build a team from the inside out that is onboard and ready to go. Jesus himself did that. He built the culture of his inner twelve disciples around the idea that they were going to make impact together. They were going to be fishers of men. They were sent out to heal and preach the Kingdom. Everything Jesus did with his disciples privately was to prepare their eventual Kingdom Impact. That should be the mentality of any church leader, and that is precisely the message that a congregation's leadership team needs to communicate.

If we return to one of the illustrations of a church making Kingdom Impact, we can see how that was done effectively. Pastor Martin Johnson, of New Beginnings Church in Peoria, IL, effectively remade the missional identity of his congregation in one dramatic meeting. On a street corner in a distressed neighborhood, he closed one chapter of his church's history and opened another. *He claimed the corner.* He confronted a church whose culture had been one that was inner-focused. They had been primarily concerned with providing the membership with a vibrant experience of worship and Bible study inside their church. But when they sought a new building, God used Pastor Johnson, and others around him, to recreate a culture of external mission and involvement in the world. In a dramatic moment, Pastor Johnson presented the future of the New Beginnings Church as a calling *to* that corner, a neighborhood that was struggling with ethnic divisions, drugs, violence, and crime. He said boldly: "God has called us here. If you want to leave you can. But you can also join this vision."

This was Pastor Johnson's Joshua moment, or his St. Crispin's Day speech, to borrow from Shakespeare's *Henry V.* In Joshua 24, Moses' successor, Joshua, son of Nun, gave the nation a choice: They could join the new mission of God's people as they acquired and settled Canaan, the land of God's promise, or conversely, they could go their own way.

> *"Now therefore fear the Lord and serve him in sincerity and in faithfulness. Put away the gods that your fathers served beyond the River and in Egypt, and serve the Lord. ¹⁵ And if it is evil in your eyes to serve the Lord, choose this day whom you will serve, whether the gods your fathers served in the region beyond the River, or the gods of the Amorites in whose land you dwell. But as for me and my house, we will serve the Lord"* (Joshua 24: 14 – 15).

Notice, Joshua's mind was made up. He was going. He was not putting this up for a vote. He was not seeing how many people would get on board before officially launching the campaign. He was casting a vision that forced a decision, either choose faithfulness and service to God, or a selfish and a "serve-us" mentality. They had to put away their idols.

That was a good reminder to me. The people who had traveled with Moses for forty years in the desert had been judged for spiritual unfaithfulness numerous times. They moved into the land of Canaan after claiming it through battle, forcing out the nations that lived by idol worship and detestable practices such as temple prostitution and child-sacrifice. The land was ready. God had been faithful. Now God needed a faithful people to settle there! As part of his St. Crispins' Day Speech, Joshua exhorted the people to put down the idols, the gods their ancestors had worshiped in Egypt. *Some of them were still worshipping idols after all that time.*

We forget that the people of God had basically lived like Egyptians for 400 years. They had a different ethnic heritage, but many of them, probably most of them, had adopted the culture of Egypt and devotion to their gods. Four hundred years is a long time. That would take us back to the early 1600s in the history of our culture in North America. That is back to the first settlements of Jamestown and Quebec City. That is how long the descendants of Abraham had lived in Egypt and were shaped by Egypt's culture.

Joshua knew, as Moses knew, that God called the descendants of Abraham and Isaac out of Egypt to be a people of his own possession. But that was not just a physical exodus. It was a mental and spiritual one as well. The exodus was the birth of Israel as a nation, the nation of God. Prior to that they were Egyptians, for all intents and purposes. Through the exodus, God introduced them to himself and to who they were really called to be — God's own people, with a mission in the world.

Idols are subtle today, but we still carry them in the church. We value position and influence, especially among fellow congregants. The longer people are in a particular congregation the more entitled they feel to be served by it. There is nothing wrong with that sentiment; the church should serve its people. We are implored to do that in Paul's Letter to the Galatians: *"Therefore, as we have opportunity, let us do good to all people, especially to those who belong to the family of believers" (Galatians 6:10).* But that is not a command to put ourselves first.

Fashioning your congregation as a team to make Kingdom Impact requires that church people address their own idolatry regarding who and what is most important. It may require a *Joshua moment* of your own where the call to follow Jesus' mission in the world is laid out clearly and people are invited to get on board. If your church has functioned for a long time as a cruise liner, where people see themselves as paying customers, cared for by a staff of employees, it is going to take some time for those idols to be set down. First, people need to recognize that they are even carrying idols. They may not know! As they do become aware, there is going to be some squirming. It is the idol, itself, that is squirming, but it will manifest in the reaction of the person carrying it. In the end, each person must personally face the decision to set the idol of self-interest down and to get on board with the mission of Jesus.

That is what we did poorly at Living Waters. There was this idea to start a community-based youth ministry and to adopt a local neighborhood to make Kingdom Impact. The leadership saw the vision along with a few key people, but for many in the congregation the vision was not fully understood or accepted as a mission of the whole church. When new kids started to show up who talked and behaved differently from the original 'church' kids, there was some confusion and fear about what was happening. It was natural. There had been no comprehensive meeting; there had been no discussion of how this might impact the church, and how those changes could be perceived by those already part of its membership. People were given no opportunity to get on board in the first place. Over time, many people adjusted and got over the surprise and eventually understood the ministry opportunity that was at hand. But the mission started when only a handful of people understood it and were behind it. It did not matter that the handful included the leaders and the pastor. It was too few to represent a true Joshua moment.

If you desire to bring this kind of change to your congregation, the first thing to realize is that it is hard to retrofit a cruise ship into a fishing boat! These are very different vessels for dramatically different purposes. Now truthfully, it is far easier to get a congregation behind a comprehensive mission to the community, than it is to retrofit a cruise ship into a fishing boat. But the relevance of the metaphor is no less important. It is going to take time, and it is going to take work, and it may also take financial investment. You cannot just steer a cruise ship into fishing waters and give everyone a fishing rod to dangle out their window! First, the people on the upper decks will never reach the water with their lines. If any fish are caught, they will get tangled in the lines of those fishing from their portholes on lower decks. And then there is the problem of what to do with the fish once they are on board. You cannot just tell everyone to pile them in their rooms for the cleaning service to take care of! Obviously, a coordinated plan is needed, otherwise there will be a lot of lines crossed and rotting fish will be everywhere. There will be quite a stink! Soon, the complaint department will receive many calls and emails, and refunds will be requested. Pastors might be familiar with that part of the metaphor too!

Preparing Your Team

At some point every metaphor outlives its usefulness and it is time to face reality, or maybe, to adopt another metaphor. How does a congregation become a "team"? Wayne Cordeiro wrote a book called *Doing Church as a Team*, published in 1998, that is still a wonderful resource for how to organize your congregation into teams of leaders. This book, along with Jim Powell's *Dirt Matters*, published in 2013, were extremely helpful to our leaders as we navigated the organizational changes necessary to orient our congregation toward mission. Jim Powell presented a compelling and insightful argument that each church must test its own "soil" to know what will grow there. Today there are so many resources, books, conferences, podcasts, and more, to assist congregational leaders to shape their vision and align their mission. Choose one that fits your context and use it. But first, let this metaphor settle in: However you get there, you need to foster an understanding in your church that you are meant to be a *team* for Kingdom Impact. Do not just create a small team or committee to do outreach. The whole congregation must on be that team in some way.

That is exactly what Jesus did with his disciples. He made them into a team. They learned from him how to live as ministers of the New Covenant; they watched him teach and heal, and then he sent them out to do the same with these instructions: *"As you go, proclaim this message: 'The kingdom of heaven has come near.' ⁸Heal the sick, raise the dead, cleanse those who have leprosy, drive out demons. Freely you have received; freely give" (Matthew 10: 7 – 8).*

Later, after he had sent out the inner twelve in this way, he sent out a larger group of disciples in groups of two with these instructions: *"He told them, 'The harvest is plentiful, but the workers are few. Ask the Lord of the harvest, therefore, to send out workers into his harvest field. ³Go! I am sending you out like lambs among wolves. ⁴Do not take a purse or bag or sandals; and do not greet anyone on the road…. Heal the sick who are there and tell them, 'The kingdom of God has come near to you'" (Luke 10: 2 – 3, 9).*

Here is how this metaphor of a team can apply to our context today. The inner twelve were prepared for a specific role in Jesus' ministry. They were to become the apostles, those who were "sent" with the message of the Gospel to the nations, as the word apostle implies in its meaning. They were also the leaders of the early church and the guardians of its message and mission. But what about the seventy-two? (some translations have seventy) A convenient way for us to interpret that is that they represent the members of your congregation. It matters not whether it was thirty-five teams of two, or thirty-six, these were people Jesus sent out ahead of him as his advance team, to prepare the way for the message. This is a vision of your congregation fashioned into a Kingdom Impact team.

If that is the local congregation in action, we must outfit this team and prepare it to be sent out in the same way that Jesus sent out the seventy-*something*. That group must be given a vision and must be equipped for the task. We know extraordinarily little about how Jesus did this. In fact, we know more about how Jesus did not equip them. The passages listed above told us they were not to be equipped with money or even footwear, for instance! A closer reading of the passage tells us they were to find a house to stay in that was owned by people of peace. While in the town, they were to heal and proclaim the Kingdom of God. If they were not welcomed, they were to brush off the dust from that town and move on. That is not extensive training by any stretch of imagination. But God was with them. They went into the towns and villages of Judea, and the Kingdom of God went before them and with them. Even the demons submitted. They walked in the authority of Jesus, as he explained when they returned from their mission (Luke 10:18).

This is the vision we can have for our congregations as they move in God's power and as they encounter the towns and villages of which they are already part. No more should we see our churches as cloistered communities, where the life of the church is conducted behind four walls, with a culture of spiritual activity hidden from the neighborhood. Instead, the vision is to become congregations that are on the move at Jesus' command:

- planting the seed of his Word in good soil,
- confronting evil on the ground,
- investing in great potential,
- changing the culture,
- revealing hidden value and worth in people, and,
- casting the broad net of God's welcome.

But how to get a congregation to think this way? How to put Jesus' Kingdom mission first? God's Word must lead the way here. People's hearts must be changed by the words of Jesus so that they see your congregation first as a mission to the world. Together, you must become students of Jesus' Kingdom vision.

Identify Key Leaders

Leaders are official by title as well as informal by influence. Official leaders are easy to identity. They will be members of a paid staff, elders or deacons, members of a church council, ministry team leaders, or small group leaders. These formal leaders must be discipled in the idea and language of mission and Kingdom Impact. That way, formal leadership teams can discuss, pray over, and act upon, Jesus' mission mandates. Small group leaders are especially key to the process. If they get behind the idea of Kingdom Impact the vision will break through into the larger congregation.

The next step is the informal leaders. These are the people whom others in the congregation look to as spiritual grandmothers and grandfathers. They play the role of mentors to those younger, or peer leaders of those who are the same age. For whatever reason, people see them as the key individuals who must also approve of the vision and direction of a congregation. The smaller a congregation is, the more prominent these informal leaders will be and the more pronounced their influence. Most often, they are fifty years of age or older, but in some cases, by force of personality, they can be younger. It is these informal leaders whose influence outlasts even those who hold offices in the church, including that of the pastor.

Carl George wrote about this in the book *Leading and Managing Your Church*, published in 1988. There he presented four groups of people that typically make up a congregation. He called them "berry buckets", (George and Logan, Leading and Managing Your Church). The key informal leaders in your congregation are the ones Carl George identified as those who predated the current pastor's tenure, and who were probably instrumental in helping to choose him or her. These informal leaders may not hold an office or a paid position, but they are as important as any of the formal leaders to build the vision of making Kingdom Impact. Warning: they may be the hardest to win over! Like it or not, they have seen many 'new' ideas come and go. They have seen the good, the bad, and the ugly, associated with the implementation of new directions and new ministries. They also have a great deal at stake in the big and small decisions that affect the congregation long-term. In many ways, they see the congregation as part of their legacy. They are not the new kids on the block.

Most likely, you know instinctively who these individuals are. Whether or not they have earned the influence they have or operated in healthy or unhealthy ways in the congregation, these spirited saints need to understand the 'why' and 'how' of any plan for Kingdom Impact. Often, it is the impact on resources that this group will think about, and ask about, first. It is not just financial resources they will be invested in, it is the human resources, the volunteers, that will be required. They themselves often represent energetic and faithful volunteers in addition to being stable sources of financial gifts to the church. The case cannot be made any clearer. These spiritual grandparents of the congregation must understand the reasoning behind efforts to impact your community for God's Kingdom. They may not agree with all the details, nor do they need to, but you want them to be able to explain why the official leaders of the church want to move this way.

Spend a few minutes writing down the names of a few key informal leaders in your congregation who must understand the vision if your church is to become a team for Kingdom Impact mission. (Beside each name, indicate a formal leader who is the key to reaching this person).

Look at the list you created above. These names represent those who influence the *air waves* in the congregation. You want the buzz in the air to be their excitement that the congregation is moving into the community to make an impact for the mission of Jesus. Consider this: the opposite would be devastating to the mission. This step is crucial to the success of building a team mindset in the congregation. If it does not occur, the risk will be that any new efforts will become the project of just a few leaders; or worse, the 'agenda' of the pastor. If that is the case, the effort will be short-lived.

Once you identify the key informal leaders that must be reached, it is important to make plans for how a Joshua moment or St. Crispin's Day speech can occur so you may bring the rest of the congregation on board. This might happen at an annual meeting, a "mission month" presentation, or the kickoff to a new program year. But whenever it occurs, it is important that the key leaders, both formal and informal, are on board and can be present for that event. Some of them should be asked to speak, to give their public support to the effort. If this can occur, the sense in the congregation will be that this is not just a passing fad, or the next "program pitch", but a cultural change moment. Remember, you risk leaving most people behind in your efforts to impact your community if you do not make this critical step.

What are you going to do to make Kingdom Impact locally?

Part of the presentation made to the congregation will have to include more than just the idea that your church will orient itself toward community or neighborhood impact for the Gospel and the mission of Jesus Christ. The message will have to include the specifics, and the specific tasks, that the members of the church will be *asked* to do. This is important, as well, if there is a financial component to the mission. Will they be asked to give only their time and talents? Or will they be asked to give of their treasure?

Before that unveiling meeting is planned, you must answer the question: What are we going to do? So, let us back up. It is time to refer to the notes you made in earlier chapters about the neighborhoods that surrounds the physical location of your church. When we did this, we used mapping software to plot the addresses of all the current members of the congregation. We saw instantly that we were not at all a 'local' church. Our congregation from its birth had been a regional church. Very few members lived within a mile of the church building. Many lived inside a circle of ten miles, but some as far as twenty or thirty or more. The glaring physical hole in the map was the circle inscribed by a mile radius around our building.

This is part of what moved us to make the effort to become a local church with a neighborhood mission. It is the reason we reached out to meet families within that one-mile circle.

This method works very well if you are a church in a city or a small town. If you are a rural church, you will have to look further out to understand the network of communities that your church is positioned to serve and impact. There might be several villages and towns that your ministry could touch, as well as farm families, or other rural residents, that see you as a local church already. As you map the area around your church, have an eye to what defines specific neighborhoods or districts. What are the issues and needs at work there? Do any of those suggest a strategy for Kingdom Impact? You might want to use county statistical information to do this in a more scientific way. Do you find mainly homeowners there, or are there many residents who pay rent? What are the income and education levels? Are there young families in newer dwellings, older residents and empty nesters in older homes, or are there neighborhoods in transition between the two?

Some churches will find that there are no local neighborhoods around their church at all, as they are in a downtown area or in an industrial or retail part of the city. If that is the case, it might be necessary to move farther out. But before you do, remember that industrial areas and stores are filled with people during the day. Is there a need felt by daytime workers? Are their childcare needs met? What do they do on their lunch breaks? Do they need a place to pray or receive counseling?

My former congregation was located right across the road from the city hall. During the season of Lent, we offered a lunchtime preaching series, where we invited city leaders to give a testimony of their personal faith and how it guided their lives and work. City workers attended these short worship services and joined us for a soup lunch afterwards. That would not have been as convenient, or even possible, if that congregation were located in the suburbs, which are largely empty during the day.

The key is to think creatively and prayerfully. Let the Spirit of God guide your discernment of the needs in the local area. Remember, God speaks through people, especially people who live in those very places you are wanting to impact. In my current congregation's work at our Jacob's Well ministry, it was an informal parents' meeting at a local restaurant that helped us tailor the program of Jacob's Well to what parents said they really needed for their children. We listened and gained partners that way. But the most important partner, of course, is God himself. What mission is he leading you to undertake? Which parable will you seek to fulfill for the Kingdom? He will tell you where the church of his Son Jesus needs to focus, and what resources are available. He will also provide resources, both financial and human to make it happen.

Once you have discovered the "lay of the land", it is time to refer to the Kingdom parables of Jesus. I believe this is a critical step. It prevents leaders from rushing too quickly, once a problem or an opportunity is identified. I say this from experience. Resist the temptation to assume that there are easy answers and solutions. Even if it feels totally clear, go back to God's Word to put your new awareness into a spiritual context. It is important to see the needs of your community through God's eyes. This will help you to understand God's call clearly. As Jesus explained in Mark 9: 28 – 29, this only comes out through prayer and fasting. (You caught me, I used that out of context). But a spiritual understanding and perspective on the needs of your community must come out, and the only way to do that is through prayer and fasting. Ask God to show it to you. Which of Jesus' Kingdom parables can you connect to what is happening in your community, and what Kingdom action will you take to make impact?

- Will you be planting in good soil you have identified?
- Will you be confronting evil on the ground?
- Will you be investing in something small to make outsized impact?

- Will you be working to make cultural change?
- Will you be uncovering hidden value and worth in people?
- Will you be casting a broad net?
- Or, is there something else you will be doing that has Kingdom value? If so, define it Biblically!

Whatever it is, make sure you are joining Jesus on his mission to renew creation in his image, and that you make this a mission of the *whole* congregation. That means that there should be a way for every age group, and every small group, to contribute to the effort. This is how that team feeling will permeate the congregation.

Telling the Story

The examples of Kingdom Impact ministries used in this book were all from the area around Peoria, Illinois. There was a reason for that. It demonstrates that the Kingdom of Jesus is active in the collective Body of Christ in *every* town and area. That is true of your town, city, or rural area, as well. Jesus promised that would be the case. The challenge now is to influence your congregation to join God's story of Kingdom Impact in a bigger way. As your chapter is written by God in partnership with your leadership, make sure you start to tell that story right away. Tell it in the context of the Biblical model you have chosen so that the glory is given back to God. Telling the story is the way in which meaning is ascribed to events.

The people of God have always done this. The ancient Hebrews were uniquely gifted at seeing the spiritual meaning associated with what was happening around them. They had prophets, inspired by God, that did this very thing. It is the reason that we have God's Word in the form we have today. God's people recorded the story of his work and mission through them. No battle was won, no evil was conquered, no mistake or error was committed, without a discernment of its spiritual meaning. That is why the Bible is filled with stories of imperfect people fulfilling the mission of God on earth. When we start to make Kingdom Impact locally, we join that bigger story of God's miraculous and transforming work.

As you see evidence of the impact of God's Kingdom through your church, tell the story to one another and to those around you: in your place of work, your school, and your neighborhood. Record it, document it, and share it. It is the chapter that God is writing with your willing and prayerful partnership. But even more joy-producing, are the stories of the lives that will be changed and transformed both inside and outside your congregation. If the story is told, it will have a life of its own, long beyond that single chapter. This is the mission of Jesus! He invites you to join it.

REFERENCES

Bennett, Daniel J. *A Passion for the Fatherless: Developing a God-Centered Ministry to Orphans.* by Pastor Daniel J. Bennett. Kregel Publications, 2014.

United Nations High Commission on Refugees, *Refugee Data Finder, July 2020, https://www.unhcr.org/refugee-statistics/*

Colson, Chuck, *Loving God.* Zondervan, Grand Rapids, MI., 1997.

Green, Michael, The Message of Matthew, The Bible Speaks Today, ed. John Stott, Intervarsity Press, Downers Grove, IL, 2000.

Kennedy, John W. *"The 4–14 Window."* *Christianity Today,* July, 2004.

Chang, Steve S. *"Don't Neglect the 4–14 Window."* The Gospel Coalition, March, 2018, https://www.thegospelcoalition.org/article/want-missional-dont-neglect-4-14-window-childrens-ministry/)

George, Carl and Logan, Robert, "Leading and Managing Your Church." Fleming H Revell Company, 1987.